The Starved

About the Author

One of the most prominent writers to grace the Odia literary scene, **Mangalu Charan Biswal** (4 May 1935–11 January 2022) was born in Pitapali, Sambalpur, Odisha. Eminent litterateur, teacher, writer, poet and noted playwright, his writings are an ode to the common man and the rich cultural heritage of Sambalpur. *Bhukha* remains his most celebrated and acknowledged work. His other plays include *Udlaa Patar Budlaa Danga*, *Luraa, Bhutiaar Hatiaar*, *Dadaar Darpan*, *Ulgulaan*, *Birsaa Bhagabaan*, *Sundar Saae*, *Chhaeli*, *Baruaa*, *Maa Samlei*, *Bir Kaahaali* and *Guri Gaa'n*.

About the Translator

Nirjharini Tripathy is an Indian writer from Odisha. She is an Associate Professor in the Department of English of Utkal University, Bhubaneswar. Her areas of research and interests include Black Studies, Caribbean Studies, African American Literature, African Literature in English, Asian American Studies, Drama/Theater and Performance Studies, Postcolonial/Decolonial, Indian Literature and Translation studies. She has authored several books and research articles in national and international publications. A few of the books authored by her are *Women and Awareness in the Writings of Manju Kapur, Mahasweta Devi and Mahesh Dattani, The Myriad Facets of Women: A Study of the Novels of Manju Kapur, Trauma and Terrorism in the novels of Don Dellilo, Mohsin Hamid and Shafi Ahmad.*

The Starved

Mangalu Charan Biswal

Translated by
Nirjharini Tripathy

hachette
INDIA

First published in Sambalpuri in 1984

This translation first published in 2023 by Hachette India
(Registered name: Hachette Book Publishing India Pvt. Ltd)
An Hachette UK company
www.hachetteindia.com

1

Illustrations in text by Harshavardhan Behura

ISBN 978-93-93701-81-7

Hachette Book Publishing India Pvt. Ltd
4th/5th Floors, Corporate Centre,
Plot No. 94, Sector 44, Gurugram 122003, India

Typeset in PT Serif 10.5/15
by InoSoft Systems, Noida

Printed and bound in India
by Manipal Technologies Limited

MIX
Paper from responsible sources
FSC™ C043100

Those who cannot remember the past are condemned to repeat it.

– George Santayana

Translator's Dedication

Jai Maa Samlei

Victory to the Goddess Samaleswari

I dedicate this book to my father,
late Dr Upendra Tripathy

I miss you Bapa

Contents

Foreword xv
Introduction 1
Pancharasi/Panchabadya 17
Dramatis Personae 22

The Starved

Scene I 35
Scene II 54
Scene III 74
Scene IV 108
Scene V 132

Glossary 135
Translator's Acknowledgements 141

Foreword

The Starved is a powerful book. Having spent my tenure in Gangadhar Meher College, Sambalpur, as a lecturer in physics from 1958 to 1965, and married to Jyotsna Rani Dash, who is from Sambalpur, I could very well relate to and feel the heart-rending story of the Bajnias (folk musicians) portrayed in this play. The dramatis personae are, in fact, representative of real-life characters that I encountered in my days at Sambalpur. It is devastating to see such talented people experience anguish, pain and suffering. The play is highly intricate with many layers of complex themes such as hunger, dying art and artists, the decline of folk music and musicians, depression, melancholy, exclusion, untouchability, caste discrimination and the status of women in the lower classes of society.

The nation had a remarkable journey of growth in the last few decades towards the advancement of society's backward sections. This play, however, subtly hints at many paradoxes and issues that the country is still facing after decades of the play's conception and 75 years of Independence. It envisions and alludes to a perfect world in which caste and class are irrelevant, and depicts the struggle between tradition and modernization.

Tradition is the foundation or root of our modern world. This book advocates for the progress towards modernity along with the revival of our dwindling culture, tradition and folk music to strengthen our roots. It also depicts the struggles, joys, togetherness and daily existence of such folk musicians in rural places. The play discusses traditional folk instruments, folk songs, folk music, plays, pastorale, traditional ballads, melodies, warbles, religious songs, tunes and lyrics.

By translating *Bhukha* into English, the translator, Dr Nirjharini Tripathy, has successfully introduced the Sambalpuri language and culture to a national and international readership. Here, there is an ineffable and perennial belief in life in these challenging times, coming from a sensitive and knowing soul. Her choice of words screams unrelenting hope and repeated emphasis on the importance of humanity, and the choice of breaking man-made barriers and uniting humanity in peace and harmony. The precious insights gained by reading Dr Tripathy's words are powerful enough to be a surrogate of the human experience itself – the same embodied processes that make the human experience meaningful by hankering to break the walls that divide mankind and build bridges. The philosophical nature of her words, choice of language and intention of reaching out to the world by translating this profound play contributes to the rich tapestry of English literature. It has a humane touch of gathered and personal knowledge of human experience with real moral and social value. It engages a meaning-making process that underpins our understanding of the world more broadly and is simultaneously questioning and investigating our limiting beliefs. Dr Tripathy has successfully captured the essence of the play and the energy of what Dr Mangalu Charan Biswal is trying to convey. It illustrates her indelible grasp of the English language as well as her native Sambalpuri language.

Jayanta Mahapatra
Fellow, Sahitya Akademi

Introduction

Set in the 1980s in the rural landscape of undivided Sambalpur, and divided into five scenes, *The Starved* portrays the plight of the Bajnias (professional folk musical instrumentalists in villages of Sambalpur, who play traditional folk musical instruments called Pancharasi or Panchabadya). In the traditional rural setting, this music was played only by members of the Harijan caste known as Ganda in Sambalpur, the (formerly) untouchables, scheduled caste people of Sambalpur. Thus, this music was also known as Ganda baja. In the urban setting, this music is called Dulduli.

It is a traditional regional instrumental orchestral folk music of western Odisha. This orchestra is an ensemble usually comprising five traditional folk musical instruments played by different Bajnias. These five instruments are Dhol, Nissan, Tasa, Jhanj and Muhuri. Folk music is incomplete without any of these instruments. In this orchestral folk music, all these musical instruments are played together simultaneously in tune and rhythm.

This music represents a primordial power in the village system of western Odisha. This power is because of the harmony of the folk instruments, their rhythms, the divine strength of the rhythms and of the socially marginalized Bajnias.

This music is endowed with divine authority in western Odisha's traditional culture. Humans and gods are linked by it. According to the local belief system, this music, the instruments, and their rhythms are thought to reflect the sermons of local goddesses. Their voices are represented through the rhythms. These Bajnias serve as a conduit for connecting people to the divine, if rhythms are the voice of the goddesses. All social, religious, and cultural occasions, such as marriage, rites and rituals to the gods and goddesses, festivals, gatherings, birth rituals, and funerals, include this music as a vital component. It links local neighbourhoods, individuals, and locations. Thus, this music serves as a means of establishing connections not just with gods but also with other people.

It provides a form of ethnic awareness and regional and cultural identity through its intense psychic rhythms that connects us with our region, regional beliefs, and identities. In other words, it represents regional and cultural inclusiveness and strengthens cultural interconnectedness. It reinforces the spirit of regional ethnicity, distinctiveness, cultural self-awareness and self-esteem.

Following the development of this folk music and reading this play, we learn that the Bajnias performed for the local political elite, including kings and landowners, in addition to all the village's social, religious, and cultural occasions. Bajnias have been supported by kings or local landowners (Zamindars and Gauntias) since pre-colonial and colonial times.

The Bajnias are the male traditional performers that play the different folk musical instruments, such as Dhol, Nisan, Tasa, Jhanj and Muhuri. In the old traditional regional perspective, these Ganda musicians were considered 'untouchable' because Dhol, the musical instrument that they play, is made from cowhide. As they are in physical contact with cowhide, they are categorized as impure and thus 'untouchable'. However, while playing this music in the ritual performances, with the powerful rhythms of the instruments, they are supposed to be directly communicating with the divine powers of the goddesses and thus these socially marginalized Bajnias become spiritually and culturally more powerful than anyone in the village. The music gives these musicians a modicum of recognition and importance in the society.

The play describes the story of five Bajnias, playing five distinct traditional musical instruments that are their main sources of sustenance. In an unnamed village of Sambalpur, they struggle to earn a livelihood due to a drop in demand. Traditional music was already in danger of dying out due to the modern musical bands with their new, advanced instruments. The struggle these artists had to overcome in order to exist is chronicled in this play over a lengthy, tragic period. The development of modern music and its new, alluring mechanical musical instruments, as well as poverty, caste prejudice and illiteracy are some of the ruthless deterrents to their progress. Folk musicians find it difficult to get jobs because people prefer modern music, therefore they are forced to find other menial professions to make ends meet. Due to their inability to build a successful business or generate income from playing traditional music, as well as the fact that they lacked any farmland or other means of agricultural production, these musicians were unwittingly at the landlord's mercy and dependent on the wages from agricultural labour and other menial tasks performed at the homes of the landlord and other upper caste members.

The community is also experiencing a drought, which lowers the need for music. The play touches on how miserable it is for farmers when there is absolutely no rain. They are on the verge of starvation due to the widespread drought and burnt farmlands. The instrumentalists believe that it was god's intention for them to be born into adversity. They interpret this situation as their destiny or karma. They lack education, and are powerless and ignorant of their rights.

The primary topics addressed in this play include hunger, the death of art and artists, and the decline of folk music and performers. The work also addresses despair, melancholy, exclusion, untouchability, caste prejudice, classism, the condition of women in lower levels of society, and a failed love relationship between a man from a higher caste and a girl from a lower caste. The joys, camaraderie, and daily lives of folk musicians in rural areas are also depicted in detail.

The Starved mainly focuses on the dilemma between embracing modernity and retaining cultural values , and the dreadful effects of the caste system and poverty. Modernism and traditional practices and heritage are merged in this drama. Throughout our history and culture, folk music has played a significant role. Folk music once had the healthiest group of supporters and listeners, who cherished and relished the music as food for their souls, and had spiritual sentiments to uncover the mysteries of human existence and its connection to the cosmos. Modernization is essential, but to advance in that direction and, more significantly, to maintain that modernity, we must reinforce our foundation. All countries with rich histories and traditions are afflicted by this issue; it is not just a problem in Sambalpur, Odisha, or India in general.

Culture, as seen in the play, is an ongoing debate between the characters as a set of deeply rooted and patterned beliefs, attitudes, values and behaviours. The definition of culture in the play, as a whole, shows that it isn't static and unchanging – it is negotiated and develops over time. Thus, in this changing time and culture, we must carefully and consciously decide and accept what is most helpful for elevating everyone's consciousness and preserve it, while discarding everything that will obstruct society's advancement. This very idea also highlights that culture is something that is learned, which supports the relevance of passing on knowledge to the following generation in a selective manner in order to have a beneficial influence on them. The world's various civilizations can be brought together through this book.

In the book, an ideal society in which caste and class are inconsequential and everyone is unified is envisioned and alluded to. A circumstance in which there is no disparity between the rich and the downtrodden; no one will have more, and no one will have little.

The five main dramatis personae in the play are Aentha, Maharagu, Hadu, Paltu and Gahadu. Aentha plays Muhuri and is the main artist in the musical troupe. He is also known as Muhuria, per the instrument, Muhuri, that he plays. Maharagu plays Dhol and thus, villagers also call him Dhulia. Hadu plays Tasa, Paltu plays Nisan and Gahadu plays Jhanj. The story revolves around the depredations and the tragic life of poverty and starvation of each of these people.

These five musicians are portrayed in the play as victims of great poverty, and caste and class prejudice. In India, where the caste system is endogamous and each caste continues to practise its inherited occupational speciality, there is widespread social stratification and hierarchy. Their rank, authority and place in the system are determined by their caste. The subcategories within the caste (or varna system) include brahmin, kshatriya, vaishya, and shudra. The shudras are perceived as being filthy, unclean, outsiders and outcasts by upper-caste society. The caste system historically places the so-called untouchables at the bottom, with brahmins at the top. The rigid divisions and sub-divisions, the dialectics of high-low, purity and defilement, and the stigma of untouchability, discrimination and disadvantages are to blame for the fracturing of Indian society.

Even though untouchability was officially prohibited when India adopted its constitution in 1950, discrimination against Dalits remained widespread. In many parts of India, the enforcement of laws intended to protect Dalits are lax, if not non-existent. Untouchability is most prevalent in rural areas, where 80 per cent of the population lives. There, Hinduism's ritualistic practices and superstitions predominate.

The placement of the musicians' homes in the village, which are situated outside of the settlement of the higher so-called clean caste, indicates that the stigma of untouchability keeps these musicians away from the upper castes. Such communities are known as para in the villages of Sambalpur. The various castes, as a result, have their distinct settlements. The dwelling or the settlement of the 'Ganda' is called Ganda para. The lower classes are avoided wherever they exist, both physically and socially. In addition to providing music for important occasions and local customs, they work in the farms as labourers and in the houses as servants of the Gauntias, Zamindars and upper caste people. They are also asked to do menial jobs. Ironically, they are in poverty despite giving music and amusement to others.

The play's musicians are made to feel as inconsequential as the farm's pebbles and as isolated from society as social lepers. Due to the belief that they belong to an impure caste, they are not allowed to use the same water source as upper-caste Hindus. Their community typically has a well, a small pond and a stream nearby for bathing, washing clothes and other uses from which the upper castes do not draw water from. If the hamlet only has one water source, these people are then given a specific area of the well, pond, stream, or river as they are not allowed to share space with people from other castes. Even though these practices are not widespread in contemporary India, it is nonetheless advisable to educate the next generation about the horrors that people have inflicted upon one another and to remind the current generation not to repeat the past.

India had the zamindari system under the British administration and the feudal system governed the villages. They were abolished with Independence, but in some areas the feudal system's power, status and authority continued for a long time. This socio-political mechanism was for the efficient administration, operation and maintenance of order in the village.

The musicians in the play rely on and live at the mercy of the upper-caste people. For many years, the village landowners had been in charge of them. In the play, Aentha reveals how parents of these musicians worked for the landlord Dina and ultimately passed away while doing so. Like their parents, they also work for Dina and continue to struggle with a mountain of debt.

Asim, an educated man and a researcher, comes to the village for his fieldwork, as he is writing a book on traditional folk music and the life of the poor musicians in the village. These musicians in the play are illiterate. When they meet Asim, they adore him and call him Pathua babu (a respectful title or form of address for a man, especially an educated one). A learned person is almost like a god to them. By maintaining this term consistently till the end of the play, the playwright Biswal intends to emphasize the issue of illiteracy, ignorance and innocence of the poor musicians and highlights the importance of education in improving the condition of the musicians. Asim becomes sentimental towards the adversities of these musicians and promises to print their pictures, names and plight in his research report, vowing to send it to the government.

Aentha harbours only one wish in life, and that is to get his only sister Kasturi married. Kasturi, meanwhile, falls in love with Asim. Asim also expresses his love for Kasturi and his desire to marry her. Aentha could not believe it because of his caste and class perceptions. Asim completes his research in the village and leaves with the promise to return and marry Kasturi. The musicians have high hopes that Asim will come back and rescue them from their wretched life. They start seeing him as a divine light, a ray of hope, who can free them from their suffering and pain.

To highlight Aentha's deplorable financial situation, the author meticulously details his home. Most of the action in this play takes place on the verandah, an outdoor area, located beneath the thatched roof of Aentha's mud home. It is primarily utilized from morning through the night for the majority of household tasks, including sitting and sleeping.

The musicians and their families use locally accessible forest materials, such as bamboo, wood, mud, wooden poles, grass, straw and date palm leaves to build their homes. Cow manure, lime clay and red soil are used to plaster the walls and floors. Aentha's house has mud walls and straw thatch, no back doors or windows and just small holes in the walls for light and airflow. As a result, the interior of the house is perpetually dark, signifying the darkness that shrouding their lives.

Aentha, in the play, has not been able to afford to buy a frock and a saree for his daughter and sister for years. The play also reveals the destitute way of living and clothing of these musicians. They wear outfits made of simple coarse, cheap handloom fabric. The women mostly wear a saree without any undergarments, blouses and petticoats. The men wear a dhoti (a piece of loincloth) covering the waist to the thigh. However, during occasions and gatherings, they wear a vest and carry a gamuchha (towel) on their shoulder. Their poor economic situation compelled them to have simple eating habits. Their main source of food is paddy, so they consume rice and pakhala (watered rice) for all three meals of the day. However, there were numerous occasions when these artists were unable to provide for their family's basic needs, let alone a single meal. Even this bare minimum requirement – a handful of food and a piece of clothing – is not available to them at times.

They are acutely aware of shadows looming over them, and everything appears dark and gloomy. At social events, someone from somewhere may occasionally ask them to provide music on specific occasions for a pittance. They often wonder how long they will be able to perform this type of folk music because it is becoming unpopular. They spend all of their earnings before nightfall due to their low income.

Addiction and poverty have a complicated relationship. Some people argue that alcohol consumption is a coping response to stress. As poor people are particularly exposed to stressful life events, many respond by increasing their consumption of alcohol and becoming 'problem drinkers'. The play presents both sides of poverty. Although those with lower incomes are somewhat more likely to struggle with drug or alcohol consumption, this does not always imply that addiction is brought on by poverty. Poverty increases stress-related problems, one of which is addiction. Addiction, in turn, exacerbates financial problems. It is a vicious circle.

Aentha suffers from tuberculosis and dies at the end of the play because of poverty and excessive drinking. There is no restriction on the Gandas on drinking liquor and smoking, from a moral, ethical or religious point of view. Mostly, they are prone to drinking in excess. A major portion of their income is spent on their drinking and offering drinks to others. They prepare liquor at home from fermented rice, fermented wild flowers and fruits of Mohul (*Madhuca longifolia*), or from fermented date palm fruits, which are freely available in the forests. On certain occasions, they buy and drink branded and distilled liquors. They smoke bidi or pica made of tobacco leaves, which are again freely available in the forests. People from all backgrounds and classes take drugs and alcohol for many reasons: for pleasure, to treat physical or emotional pain, for stress or anxiety, or because their friends do. Enough research shows that the pattern of who develops a drug/alcohol problem and encounters other problems has a close link between addiction and social exclusion.

Another curse on these people is illiteracy. Functionally illiterate parents frequently prioritize work over education and their children are more likely to follow in their footsteps. Illiterate adults are more vulnerable to illness, exploitation and human rights violations. This creates a generational cycle of disadvantage. Aentha suffers from tuberculosis, and Kasturi takes him to the village witch doctor in the hope that he can be cured with black magic. Though belief in black magic is not always associated with illiteracy, poverty may be a factor. They are forced to resort to black magic because they cannot afford to see a doctor.

They worship Hindu gods and goddesses and believe in supernatural powers. They usually worship a local deity, known as the Goddess of Power. Natural elements such as the Sun, Moon, Earth, water, air, trees and stones are also revered. Despite their evident misery and desolation, they are rooted in Indian tradition and culture. Their devotion is unfazed by their poverty or ill-treatment at the hands of society. Though they have not read the texts, they have acquired this knowledge through folk songs. In their conversation, we come across many references to the Ramayana and Mahabharata.

The human condition is poignantly but insightfully represented in this play. Asim, the educated young man, was the only ray of hope for these Bajnias. They had faith that he would return to rescue them from their plight. Aentha was hoping that Asim would marry his sister Kasturi so that he could die in peace. Kasturi waited for her love to return and marry her. However, at the end of the play, they learn that Asim will not be able to return because he has been arrested by the police. These people were unsure of the reason, however, they believe it was his writings on the discrimination between rich and poor that must have displeased the government. Kasturi, Aentha and the musicians were devastated by this news. Their dreams, desires and hopes all rested on Asim. Aentha died prematurely as a result of his disease, unable to bear the burden of responsibility for his sister and daughter, and extreme poverty.

When Phula asks her aunt for food (in the last scene of the play), despite being aware that her father has died, the play comes to a tragic end. Living in survival mode leaves her numb, and she approaches her father's passing pragmatically, her hunger for food overpowering her emotions and desentisizing her to suffering and agony.

Illiteracy, addiction, poverty and caste prejudice are challenges faced by those working to preserve the vanishing folk music genre. For humanity, it serves as a wake-up call. The world wasn't as conscious of the years of collective victimhood and agony that subjugated lower-caste members endured in silence until socio-religious reform movements gave them a platform for their collective expression of discontent and unrest. Members of these communities frequently turned to folk rituals for a cathartic release of transgenerational and communal victimhood and trauma since they lacked socially acceptable means of expressing their sense of injustice and anguish. Such hidden pain has significant, intricate and dynamic effects on both the individual and interpersonal levels.

Trauma has a terrible effect when expression, healing and integration are denied. The characters in the play are denied basic human rights, such as the right to a decent life, the right to equality, the right to basic amenities and the right to be respected, all because they are born into a particular caste. The characters in the play are victims of the societal construct of the caste system. For instance, Kasturi, in the play, like any other girl and as an individual, has the desire to dress well and eat well. She wants to wear new and beautiful sarees during festivals in the village. However, her poverty denies her such privileges. She tells her brother

Aentha that she wants to cry her heart out sitting behind closed doors inside the house. She was not even sure of her relationship with Asim and could not express her feelings to anyone, fearing she might not be accepted by the community or Asim since she is lowborn. Aentha always wanted to give his sister and daughter a dignified and privileged life. However, he is unable to do so. Being aware of the fact that his sister Kasturi is a very pretty girl and deserves a very good husband from a well-to-do family, he feels helpless because of the fact he is poor and lowborn. His parents had gone through the same pain and sufferings, and now even he endures torments. He could not even heal from the pain that has been going through generations. The situation is almost the same with most of the musicians in the play. Their caste does not allow them to integrate themselves with the other people in the village. They are treated as insignificant, inconsequential, and isolated from society. Poverty makes it impossible for them to lead a better life. This leads to trauma and depression, which is felt in all these musicians in the play. Hadu, Paltu, Gahadu and Maharagu are all victims of poverty.

In addition to endorsing all of the system's worst and most despised practices, such as exploitation, untouchability, slavery, humiliation, discrimination, and ostracism of lower caste members, the society also added additional elements to these practices, such as severe punishments for violating these norms, purification rituals, atonements, and so on. Dina asks the musicians if they have forgotten his beatings.

This has been going on for generations as depicted in the play. Aentha tells Dina that his father and mother both died while serving Dina. They could never raise their voice against him. After them, it is he who is serving him.

Though the play ends with the tragic death of Aentha, it gets more despondent when Phula asks her aunt for food, unmindful of her father's death as her hunger overpowers her emotions and loss. Yet, at this point, Kasturi, though engulfed in poverty, loss, loneliness and helplessness, faces the situation stoically. She doesn't show her worry, rather answers sensibly and goes to the house to give food to Phula. She takes over the responsibility of the house and her niece after the death of her brother, who was the only food provider and support to the family. Dina, the wealthy person in the village, offers his support to the deceased family and goes to the extent of saying that he will be a brother to Kasturi and will take care of the family till the time he is alive. This gives moral and emotional support to her. The play, therefore, presents the social nature and the affirmation of the bonds that the village people share among themselves. It brings out the social virtue of human solidarity in the village community. Thus, the plays ends on a note of resilience and celebrates the irrepressible human will to survive in the face of grief, adversity and starvation.

Pancharasi/Panchabadya
Five Musical Instruments in the Play

Dhol is a large and long double-sided wooden drum/ barrel with a length ranging from 90 cm to 1.5 m. It is a membranophone that produces music by striking or rubbing the membrane. It is the leading instrument in Pancharasi. The two open ends (left and right) of the Dhol are covered completely with strips of stretched cowhide. The Dhol also has strings fastened from left to right. These skins can be stretched, tightened or loosened with the help of the interwoven strings. Stretching and tightening the cowhide is done frequently to produce a better pitch of the sound. The stretching on both sides also helps in regulating the high- and low-frequency bass sound produced by striking both ends of the instrument. The instrumentalist carries the Dhol over his shoulder, suspended from the neck with the help of a cotton strap.

Nisan is a musical instrument with a broad top and tapered bottom. It is a membranophone where the body of the instrument is made of wood and iron sheets. The top rounded part is made of cowhide. Sound is produced by striking this part with two sticks. Similar to the Dhol, it is slung over the shoulder, suspended from the neck by a cotton strap. The music produced booms like a rumble of thunder and is heart throbbing, symbolizing the strength of the goddess.

Tasa is a musical instrument whose body is made of clay. Its size is comparatively smaller to the Dhol and Nisan. It has a broad top tapered towards the base. The top is covered with a strip of cowhide. It is a membranophone that produces sound by striking the top leather string with two sticks. It produces the sound of fear and powerful emotions that embodies the divine power of the goddess. Even this is carried around the neck by the instrumentalist.

Jhanj is a pair of concave metal plates, or cymbals, usually made of brass, bronze, or iron. They are tied to each other with straps of thick cotton threads. It produces a clashing rattle sound when the metal plates are struck against one another. It is connected to the divine as its sound is similar to the sound of the bells in temples.

Muhuri is a musical instrument with the shape of a short and narrow pipe or tube. It is made of wood. The end of the pipe or instrument is made of metal with a conical shape. It produces sound when air is blown in it from the top through its reed. The instrumentalist gently holds it in both hands, takes it to the mouth, and blows air through it in various tunes. The sound is considered auspicious in all festivals and rituals. Muhuri plays the role of giving a voice to the music. It produces a kind of soothing tune.

The Five Musical Instruments

Dhol

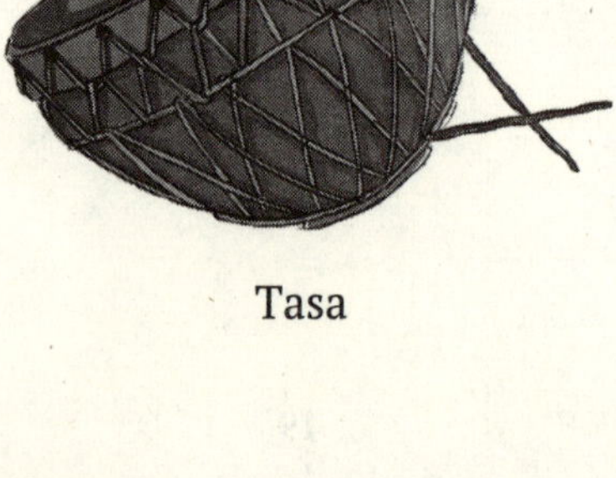

Tasa

Nisan

Jhanj

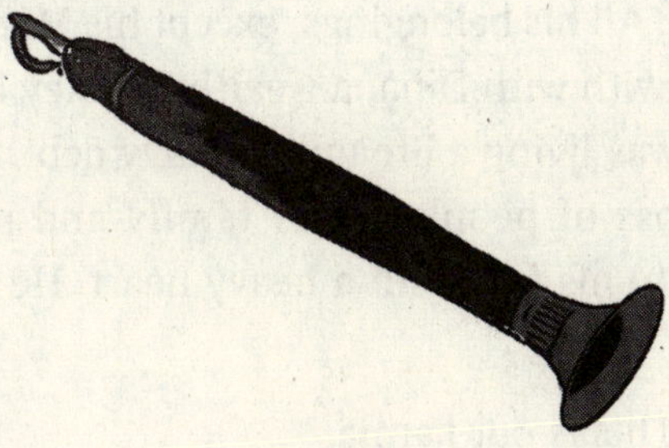

Muhuri

Dramatis Personae

Aentha

Aentha, the protagonist, belonging to the Bajnia community, plays a major role in the play. He plays the musical instrument Muhuri and hence is mostly called by other musicians as Muhuria. He is a widower with one marriageable sister named Kasturi and a daughter named Phula. Aentha's parents died when Kasturi was a child, leaving her to Aentha. His wife died after giving birth to Phula. Thus, he becomes a father to both the girls, Kasturi and Phula. If losing his parents and wife was a tragedy in his life, another suffering was poverty. All his belongings, except his Muhuri, were on a mortgage with with Dina, a wealthy money lender of the village. He was living a life under heavy debt. He accepted both, the loss of people in his family and poverty, and succumbed to his fate with a heavy heart. He mentions in the play:

Aentha: This is our karma.
What can be done?

He is a well-built person with a muscular body. He is a responsible person who takes care of his family and his musical troupe as well. He is very affectionate, considerate, and sensible. He understands his responsibility towards his sister Kasturi and takes care of her by playing the role of a father in her life. He dreams of getting his sister married to a nice person and with a grand celebration. He also desires to give a privileged life to Kasturi and his daughter Phula. He never made Phula feel the absence of a mother in her life. His father and mother worked for the wealthy Dina in the village and died while serving him. He is an honest and genuine person, which is evident from the kind of trust and faith Dina and the other musicians have in him. He plays the role of a leader amongst the musicians. He takes most of the decisions in their group. His credibility is revealed to the readers when we observe that all the musicians listen and obey him. Dina trusts him. However, Aentha – despite all his good qualities – becomes the victim of poverty and illness. He could not even afford to buy a frock for his daughter Phula. The following dialogue between father and daughter in the play reveals Aentha's helplessness:

Phula: You have to buy me a new frock this Puspuni, father.

Aentha: (*to himself*) Well, if I get some money, only then can we buy one.

Phula: Look father, this frock is torn.

Aunt stitched it, but it tore again at the same place like a wide-open mouth.

Aentha: (*cuddles Phula*) Dear, everything for us is going to be a hungry wide-open mouth.

His tragic life addicted him to drinking and smoking, leading him to his death. Though he was taking great care of his family, he cursed himself thinking he failed to give his sister and daughter a good life.

Maharagu

Maharagu, another musician, plays the musical instrument Dhol and is thus named Dhulia by others in the group. His instrument is considered the main in the troupe, as Paltu speaks about Maharagu and his dhol in scene I of the play:

Paltu: What can one do with just the Nisan?
'For what is music without a drum,
And what is a king without a kingdom!'

Despite his talent and skill as a great musician, he suffers from poverty and leads a wretched life. He mentions in the play:

Maharagu: You know what a wretched life I lead.
If I open my underfed mouth, you can see all my thirty-two teeth jutting out.

He was married to a beautiful, charming and bubbly young girl and blessed with a child, leading a happy life. But his happiness was for a short while, as he lost his child and his wife went into depression, becoming lifeless. Poverty and the death of the child left him helpless and melancholic. Though he is quite young, he looks old because of his miserable life. Paltu says about him in the play:

Paltu: Look at brother Maharagu, how does he look like he does?
Is he as old as he appears to be?

Hadu

One of the five musicians, Hadu plays the Tasa. We understand Hadu to be realistic and logical even though he suffers from destitution. He says in the play:

Hadu: Even if we don't have a handful of rice at home, we need to find it from somewhere and feed our children.

He is in heavy debt to Dina. He is warned by Dina in the play:

Dina: Haebo Hadu, do you even keep an account of the payments that you owe me?
You paupers, how much can I give you on credit?

He is illiterate and admits that he is to blame for his lack of literacy. He does not blame anyone else or even his fate for his miserable life. Rather, he blames himself. He realized that because he never paid attention to his studies as a child and wasted time. It was time to face his karma now. In the play, he tells Dina:

Hadu: (*looks at the letter*)
But, what shall I do with it?
It is like playing music for the deaf.

Hadu: Whether it is in your luck or not, is a different matter.
I was dull and lethargic in my studies from the beginning, I always made excuses for stomachaches and headaches to escape from my studies.

Hadu: Life is playing pranks on me today for the pranks I played on life in childhood.

Gahadu

In the play, Gahadu is a musician who plays the Jhanj. He is one of those impoverished musicians. He does not even have a handful of rice. He recognizes their helpless situation. He understands that they cannot earn more money with traditional musical instruments. They work very hard for a small amount of money, and whatever they earn is gone by the evening. In the play, he says:

Gahadu: Where to search and how to fetch 'that handful'?

Gahadu: Each day is misery in the life of a poor person!
We break our spines just to earn a paltry sum of money.

Paltu

In the play, he plays Nisa. He is a poor musician who feels the pain and problems of his fellow musicians. He also realizes that whatever money they make from playing music is insufficient to feed their hungry stomachs. In the play, he expresses sympathy for the other musicians and says:

Paltu: Only a destitute can feel the pain of another destitute.

Kasturi

In the play, she is Aentha's sister. She was a child when her parents died. Her brother takes care of her. He acts as both her father and mother. She wishes to dress nicely for festivals. Their poor condition, on the other hand, kills her desires. She is a lovely and affectionate young lady. She looks after her brother and niece. She is constantly concerned about her brother's health. She is aware of his drinking and smoking habits. She makes every effort to convince Aentha to give up alcohol and bidi. She realized that if this addiction took Aentha's life, she would be left alone with the responsibility of her niece, who is a child. She says:

Kasturi: I see darkness everywhere.

If anything, unfortunately, were to happen to my brother, how would I live?

The very thought drowns me in misery. (*screams softly*)

Kasturi: You know my plight!
My brother is sick.
My niece is a small child.
We don't even have a handful to eat.

She falls in love with an educated man named Asim, who visits their village from a city for research purposes. They agree to marry, however, her dream of marrying Asim is dashed when he is apprehended by the police and does not return to the village at the end of the play. Aentha dies, and she is left alone to care for her niece.

Phula

She is Aentha's daughter and a child in the play. Her mother dies shortly after she is born. Her father and aunt, Kasturi, look after her. She is portrayed as a child who yearns for good food and a frock, both of which she is denied. At the end of the play, she loses her father.

Dina

He is the wealthy money lender in the village, and his name, Mahajan, means wealthy. He owns many agricultural lands as well as a grocery store. He is tired of lending money to the village's poor musicians. He lends them money but keeps their possessions on mortgage. These musicians are of great assistance to him in his time of need. They have served him and his forefathers for several generations. They work as labourers on his agricultural land as well as in his house. At one point in the play, he speaks harshly to them out of rage and frustration, even threatens to kick them out of the village and auction their homes because they were not paying his outstanding account but calms down and asks for forgiveness later. He is the one who feeds these hungry mouths and stands by them in their hour of need. When Aentha dies at the end of the play, he consoles Kasturi and promises to look after her as if she were his sister. He says:

Dina: (*sees Kasturi crying*)
Dear Kasturi,
Why do you cry?
Your brother died and left you behind, does that mean you will keep crying like this?
Am I not a brother to you?
Why do you worry till the time I am alive?
Wealthy Dina is here for you.
You have everything.

Asim

Asim is a young, learned man, researching on traditional folk music and musical instruments. He comes to the village to collect data on the traditional Sambalpuri music and gather information on the lives of these musicians. He spends some time with these musicians in the village and eventually understands their poverty-stricken life. He is deeply affected by the deprived living conditions of such talented people and tries to mention it in his book. Thereby, wanting to elevate their condition through the support of the government. He appears to be the only educated person amongst the illiterate musicians and thus had been referred by them as 'Pathua babu' throughout the play.

Asim: My research is on the poor, wretched, deprived, underprivileged and backward people of the society.

The society we live in comprises of some people who are rich and others who are poor: the haves and the have-nots.

I am a 'Bhukha' and I am in search of all the Bhukhas like me in this society. I want to understand and get a feel of their customs and culture, life and living, happiness and sorrows. What can be done so that we can all become one? And can live our lives by sharing with each other. No one will have surplus and no one will have less.

He expresses his love for Kasturi and his desire to marry her. He completes his research in the village and leaves with the promise to come back and marry Kasturi. Aentha was hoping that Asim would marry his sister Kasturi so that he could die in peace. Kasturi waited for her love to return and marry her. Asim says:

Asim: (*hugs Kasturi*)

I am giving you my word, Kasturi.

> Whether I get a job or not, I will come back to you for sure.
>
> I am not that great a man as you think, Kasturi.
>
> I am just a normal human being like all of us here.
>
> Kasturi, I swear on you, I swear on myself, I swear on anybody you say I will come back to you, surely.
>
> I will put vermilion on your forehead and bangles on your hands, and I will marry you.

These illiterate, poverty-stricken musicians started seeing Asim as their God Ramachandra, their saviour who could liberate them from their wretched life. He was the only hope for them. They kept waiting for him to return after submitting his research documents to the government. They were sure that the government would understand their plight through the writings of Asim and do something for them. However, it didn't fructify. Their hopes were shattered as they learned that Asim could not return because the police arrested him.

The Starved

Scene I

(*Dusk. Hadu and Paltu are sitting in the verandah, under the eaves of Muhuria's thatched roof. A Nisan and a Tasa are kept nearby.*)

Hadu: Haebo Paltu!

Paltu: What is it?

Hadu: Nothing much to say, but is it not a very pleasant night?

Pick up your Nisan and let's play some music.

Paltu: What can one do with just the Nisan?

'For what is music without a drum,

And what is a king without a kingdom!'

Hadu: Usually Maharagu comes here around this time every day. What happened to him today?

He is a strange fellow.

Paltu: Do you say he is just strange? He is the laziest of the lazy.

Maharagu: (*arrives with the Dhol hanging from his shoulder*)
You scoundrels, why do you scorn me?
Do you think I can't hear you?

Hadu: Who is stopping you? We obviously wanted you to hear us.
Now clean your ears with warm oil and listen to every word we say about you.

Paltu: Haebo Maharagu, couldn't you come a little earlier? We are fed up of waiting for you.

Maharagu: (*tightens the strings of the Dhol*)
Even if I want to come early, how can I?
You know what a wretched life I lead.
If I open my underfed mouth, you can see all my thirty-two teeth jutting out.
Only after I manage to get hold of a handful of rice from somewhere and cook myself a meal, can I step out.

Hadu: We all suffer the same fate, brother.
Which one of us has the luxury of rice stored in hay granaries like that wealthy Dina?

Paltu: You son of a gun, Hadu! You are right.
Only a destitute can feel the pain of another destitute.

Hadu: Even if we don't have a handful of rice at home, we need to find it from somewhere and feed our children.

Maharagu: You are being silly, Hadu. You are a barren childless couple; you don't seem to be in any problem with too many mouths to feed.

You can satisfy your food cravings with all the rich fancy foods you wish to have. However, you know my plight. Don't you?

Hadu: I know, but then...

Maharagu: What is this 'but'? You know my case very well.

Hadu: But then, what I meant to say is, is your wife not at home?

Maharagu: Well, she is at home, but then, her presence and absence seem to be the same.

You know that she is always sick, always panting.

Ask her to finish a job quickly, and the poor girl, she will be dead.

She seems ever fatigued and wearied.

Paltu: Health and well-being is inconsistent, brother.

Every day is not the same.

Maharagu: You are right, nevertheless, hers is a different case.

Earlier, she was a charming and bubbly young lady

After we lost our child, she has become lifeless.

You have seen her in her better days, haven't you?

Hadu: Yes! Such is life, sometimes you can't have your cake and eat it too.

Time and situation are not steady.

Fate changes as and when god wishes it to!

Paltu: Haebo, how do you manage to always speak the right thing, the right way and at the right time. From where did you learn all this wisdom?

Maharagu: You were hurrying me, whereas that rascal Gahadu has not come yet.

Hadu: Let him come, meanwhile, bring your Dhol, Nisan and Tasa.

Paltu: Hadu is right! The sound of the music will bring him here.

(*Maharagu holds the Dhol, Hadu holds the Tasa and Paltu holds the Nisan and they start playing their musical instruments.*)

Gahadu: (*arrives with a Jhanj hung on his shoulder*) Great! Your music is booming.

Hadu: What are you waiting for?

Hold the Jhanj and play it.

Maharagu: What were you doing, you half-dead zombie? Don't you have any sense of days and time?

Gahadu: (*sits*) I can come only after I have had something to eat.

Maharagu: How much do you gobble? You glutton!

Handful only is all you need to tuck into your mouth.

Gahadu: For which 'that handful' too should be available, isn't it?

Where to search and how to fetch 'that handful'?

Hadu: Gahadu is right, brother.

We destitutes are in great misery,

I am fed up with this kind of life.

Maharagu: Beat the Jhanj properly.

Haebo Hadu, sing a song.

Paltu: Come on! Sing a song.

Hadu: Fine, I'll do that. You begin the music (*sings*)

Rasarkeli re-

Hey! Juicy fruit!

Here comes the spring

Sitting on the tree, the cuckoo sings.

Fragrance of the kewda flower spreads

Fair country girl on the nature trail treads.

The smiles of the nubile posse spreads

And slowly the countryman is fascinated.

I feel forlorn without you

Will die quietly silently, missing you.

(*keeps playing the instruments ceaselessly*)

Paltu: Oh!
Sing one more song –
Sing 'Dalkhai'!

Hadu: Fine, then play the music.
Dalkhai re!
Hey, eater of leaves!
Come country girls to pluck leaves
With bamboo basket Gurbari leaves.

Dear, call Janki, will go to the forest
Here, runs Janki, to go to the forest.

Oh, dear Shakuntala! Why do you lie despair?
Come soon Nura! The Sun is scorching with its flare.

Says Bhama, only young girls will go
Will be caught, if old women go.

When friends go together,
Some pluck up the mount
Some pluck down the mount.

Some fill the bamboo basket
Some leave it half filled.

Some say granny
Some say grandmother.

Spray chilly and salt
in fermented rice water.

Where is that Kenti,
Beaten by husband
her face is bruised.

Hey, eater of leaves!

(*stops playing instruments, and mops face to wipe sweat*)

Gahadu: I wonder, how much can we earn by playing music like this? What we earn in the day, we exhaust by the evening!

Maharagu: I agree, how much can one earn by playing instruments like this?

Hadu: Won't this plight of ours ever change?
Will all of us remain in this condition forever?

Gahadu: Everything feels dark and so gloomy. I constantly feel the darkness hovering over me, brother.
Sometimes, someone from somewhere may call us to play music on certain occasions with a meagre pay of two-hundred or four-hundred rupees.

Paltu: Four-hundred in total is what we earn.
When we divide that amongst us, we get a small amount.
We live an eternally penurious life.

Maharagu: How will our children survive? Tell me.
How will we pull through this hard time?
We need some more money to survive!

Gahadu: Each day is a misery in the life of a poor person!
We literally break our spines just to earn a paltry sum of money.

Paltu: Look at Maharagu dada,
How does he look like he does?
Is he really as old as he appears to be?

Hadu: Why should he appear so aged when he is quite young.
He is getting his moustache now.
Pretty virile and young enough to get another bride for himself.

Gahadu: You talk of another bride? He is drained out with just one!

Paltu: Leave such petty talks, brother.
What will we gain by stretching such pointless arguments?
We are tired after playing instruments for so long.
Ask Aentha dada to buy us some drinks.

Gahadu: You said it right.
The handful of rice we ate in the day has already been exhausted.

See, how the stomach starts growling in hunger again,

A few shots of booze may soothe these hunger pangs of our starving stomachs, brother!

Hadu: Please go call Aentha dada.

Paltu: Oh no! I am too scared of him.

Hadu: Why? Is he a tiger? Will he eat you?

Paltu: Did you call him a tiger? He is actually more dangerous than a tiger.

The way he gazes at you, it seems as if you would be buried in the netherworld.

Gahadu: You are a coward.

Paltu: Whoa! Do you think you are brave enough?

If you are that courageous, why don't you call him yourself?

Prove your point.

Gahadu: Do you think I can't call him?

Paltu: Precisely, who said you can't? Call him out.

Gahadu: See, I am calling him. (*goes to Aentha's door*)

Dada bo! Haebo dada (*all laugh*)

Aentha dada!

Kasturi: (*from inside*) He is asleep!

Gahadu: Wake him up, nuni!

Kasturi: He won't wake up; he has been sleeping for a long while.

Paltu: That's why, it will be fun, wake him.
Just one peg will make him wide awake, he won't be dull anymore.

Kasturi: (*from inside*) He mentioned that he was not feeling well,
If I wake him up, he will be furious.

Hadu: Wake him up, move him a bit.

Kasturi: Ohh no! I am so scared of him,
He just flies into a rage for no reason.

Hadu: (*to Maharagu*) If nuni is scared, then why don't you go and wake up Aentha dada.
He would never be mad at you.

Maharagu: You are making a fool of me!
If I wake him up, you all will get drinks and I will be chided!
No... no... not me!

Gahadu: Why should he scold you? What is he to us?
Is he our god?

Maharagu: Look at him!
How dare you talk like that about Aentha dada?
Such a tiny mouth, and talking so big!
You little guy, you don't know Aentha dada well, understood?

Gahadu: (*loudly*) I know him, I know him well enough.

Maharagu: Look, I am telling you Gahadu, don't yell at me like that.

Gahadu: What will you do?

Maharagu: What will I do? (*tightly slaps Gahadu twice in anger*)
This is what I can do!
You baby mice, how could you be so mouthy to me?
I will cut off your head and throw it away. Do you know that?

Gahadu: You bragger, just because I tolerate you, you think you are as strong as the bull.
Watch out! I will show you. (*leaves*)

Maharagu: What will you do?
If you say anything more, I will strangle you and drink your blood like a tiger.

Gahadu: (*screams*) Mind your tongue! I am warning you.

Maharagu: Shut up!
I have already given you two slaps.
If you say anything nasty like that again, I will give you one more such hard slap that you will remember throughout your life.

Gahadu: (*to Hadu*)

You be the witness Hadu dada, for the way he is behaving with me, if I get angry, neither Indra nor Chandra can save him. I will make it so difficult for him.

Maharagu: Look, don't hiss at me standing up on the tip of your toes like a cobra standing on its tail. I am telling you, I will rip you apart by the legs like Jarasandha.

Aentha: (*comes out of the hut, rubbing eyes*) Hey! Why are you so rowdy?

Hadu: You rascals! Keep quiet, Muhuria dada is awake.

Paltu: Brother, these idiots have made a ruckus here.

When the cat is away, the mice will play!

Why don't you guys shout now, in front of brother Aentha?

Hadu: Truly, brother! Aentha dada's entry makes everyone scared and quiet.

Aentha: Hold on, hold on. Don't shout any more.

I had a body ache so I was resting on bed.

Hadu: Right. Dada seems to be running a temperature.

Aentha: The way you are shouting, you won't let humans rest or sleep.

Hadu: Dada, you can never straighten a dog's tail.

Gahadu: (*weeps*) Dada, I didn't say anything to him.
He slapped me tightly twice.

Maharagu: What do you say, just two slaps? Ask me, I am ready to give you more.

Aentha: Oh! Do you want to show you are a bully?

Gahadu: Look, how he has beaten him.

Aentha: (*touches*) Really, seems bruised.
Haebo Maharagu,
Why are you so inhumane?
He is one of our musicians, like a blood brother.
How could you raise your hand at him?
Don't you consider this person a human?

Hadu: He is cranky. If he gets furious, he can't think of anything.

Aentha: Does he eat rice or something else?
Maharagu, what do you eat?

Maharagu: I did a mistake Guru.

Aentha: Mistake! (*to Gahadu*) You go, dear. Look, he is a puny boy; you never know you might end up doing serious damage to him? Would you want to commit murder?

Hadu: Okay, done.
Dada, we wanted to tell you something.

Aentha: What is it?

Hadu: (*to Paltu*) Tell?

Paltu: (*to Maharagu*) You tell him?

Maharagu: (*to Paltu*) Why don't you tell him then?

Aentha: Come on, tell me, what do you guys have to say?

Paltu: Well, what can we say?

I was just saying that my body is paining, and I really don't know why.

Hadu: Thus, if the body gets a few shots of liquor, I think it will feel better.

Gahadu: Hadu dada is right Guru, if this is what you suggest.

Aentha: So late in the night!

Who will go to get it?

Paltu: Hah! Dhulia dada is waiting on his toes.

Hadu: Why shouldn't he be?

Will he not get a little more than his share for his extra effort?

Paltu: Of course, why should he die of thirst? (*everyone laughs*)

Aentha: Maharagu, will you go?

Maharagu: Actually I feel lazy to go.

It is very irksome in the night.

The point is, the contractor is manageable, but his wife, the shrew, is very pesky.

Gahadu: Money is all that matters to her.
She will take money to give the stuff.
Now, what is the issue here?

Maharagu: You don't know that woman.
She is a fat she-buffalo.
If you fall short of just a twenty-five paisa payment, she is the kind to scream at the top of her voice, terrifying you enough to make you pee right on the spot.
And do you know what she says?

Hadu: What does she say?

Maharagu: (*in female voice*)
You exceeded the quantity, pour back liquor worth twenty-five paisa in the pot.
Are you pouring it back or not? (*shouting and screaming*)
(*all laugh*)

Gahadu: Such a snobbish and conceited woman!
She has not dealt with me so far.

Hadu: Aah! (*points Paltu towards Gahadu*)
Look at him...
She can store you in her karat. (*all laugh*)

Paltu: Why do you gabble?
If you want to drink, just order it. (*fatigue*)

It is the dead of night and we have to sleep as well! (*goes to the backyard of the house to pee*)

Hadu: You are right.

Who will keep waiting the whole night?

Aentha: Oh, dear Kasturi, nuni, please get up.

A five-rupee note is in the front pocket of my shirt, please give it to me.

Kasturi: (*from inside*) These people will not let us live in peace it seems.

Maharagu: Why are you so angry, nuni, please listen to what Guru says.

Kasturi: (*comes out of the house angrily*) He says rubbish and nonsense.

Aentha: There was a five-rupee note in the pocket of my shirt, nuni.

If it is there, bring it!

Kasturi: Will that five-rupee note be there in your pocket forever?

What about those pulses, matchstick, tea leaves packet and chilly that I bought with that money last evening?

I also bought yellow pipe crunch rolls of fifteen paisa for Phula?

Aentha: Aren't even one or two rupees left?

Kasturi: No, not even one or two rupees are left.

Hadu: Why in fractions, bits and pieces?
Bring all the money, whatever is there! (*all laugh*)

Kasturi: (*furious*) No bits and pieces even, nothing is left.
It is the dead of night, go back to your home and sleep.

Paltu: Few pegs would have relieved the body by the morning.

Aentha: You heard her, brothers.
I don't have any money left with me.

Kasturi: You are not well, dada.
Always coughing,
You look gaunt, the body has shrunk like a wooden door.

Maharagu: That is why I am telling you, nuni.
Few pegs would have been better for him.

Kasturi: These drunkards will kill you, brother. You know that better. (*enters home*)

Aentha: Nuni is getting furious.
Go, sleep, go.
We will see tomorrow.

Hadu: Even if you don't ask, we will leave Muhuria dada.
Without a drink, I feel like a dried fish.

Gahadu: You feel dried?
I feel soaked and saturated.

Aentha: Come on, now leave.
We will meet tomorrow.

Hadu: Haebo Paltu, let's go.
Do you still hope of getting it?

Paltu: Going... Guru...

Kasturi: Now go and sleep. (*from inside*)
You can display your epic Mahabharat tomorrow,
Brother, come inside and sleep.

Everyone: Let's go... let's go...

(*All leave. The moonlight of the full moon night passes through the hut. Aentha enters the hut. It is almost an empty, bare house. From a distance a faint song Oh darling can be heard. Researcher Asim babu arrives in a pajama and a kurta, a cotton sling bag hung on the shoulder, and a shawl wrapped around him. He looks like a learned man.*)

Asim: I will sit and rest for a while on this verandah.
I am tired of roaming. My hands and legs are fatigued.

(*spreads a cotton towel on the verandah and lays on it*)

I don't know what they will think of me! I will be dead if they beat me thinking I am a thief.

Let them think and do whatever they want to. I can at least sleep here tonight.
I will figure out the rest in the morning.

(*takes out a blanket from the sling bag, wraps it around himself and starts snoring*)

Lights fade out... The stage is completely dark.

Scene II

(*Crack of dawn. The light of day hankering to shine. Kasturi comes out of the hut to sweep the yard. She sees someone sleeping on the verandah, under the eaves of their hut, covered in a blanket from head to toe. The person cannot be seen.*)

Kasturi: From where has this fellow come?
Sleeping like a dried twig.
Hey! wake up... wake up.
I need to sweep and mop the hut and yard.

Phula: (*Phula comes out of the hut brushing her teeth with a twig*) Who is this, nana?

Kasturi: Look, I don't know from where this fellow has come, like a leaf flying in or an abandoned boat docking.
I woke him up, but he is stock-still!

Phula: (*laughs*) Look at him, nana! How is he snuggled under his blanket?

Kasturi: Haeho babu... oh lord...

Asim: (*rubbing eyes and stretching body*)

Om! Victory to Goddess Sita and God Ramchandra.

Oh! Where am I?

(*looks at Kasturi*)

Wherever maybe, at least I am among human beings!

Kasturi: Are you not yet awake, babu?

Asim: (*looks at Kasturi*)

Having caught a glimpse of your face in the morning light, I'll have a good day.

Kasturi: Stop your nonsensical talks, seize your belongings and move aside.

Let me clean the house and yard.

Asim: (*catches sight of Kasturi's beautiful face*)

Wah! Bravo, bravo, beautiful!

Kasturi: What are you blabbering like our Chaitu?

Asim: (*turns to the other side, covers himself with the blanket and sleeps*)

Kasturi: Look at him! Slouched back again like an immovable python who has swallowed a frog.

Keep sleeping, sleep.

Phula: Nana, what else shall I carry with me to the pond?

Kasturi: Bring my tiny tin box of tobacco paste girl. Also bring the small piece of rag lying in the corner, behind the door.

(Comes out of the hut clutching a mud pot on the curve of her waist. Phula brings the tobacco tin box and the rag. Kasturi stuffs a bit of tobacco paste inside her mouth and leaves.)

Keep sleeping, sleep.

Let me come back after a bath and deal with you.

(Leaves for a bath. Phula follows her. After both leave, Asim babu wakes up in a trance, pulls back the blanket from his head and sits comfortably. He looks around carefully, and then stands up and strolls around for a while. Birds chirp at the break of the day. The sound of the ringing bells and conch shell trumpets can be heard faintly from a temple. He is pleased with the surroundings. The moment he realizes Kasturi and Phula are returning, he wraps himself with the blanket and sleeps. Phula and Kasturi arrive.)

Phula: Nana, that person would have woken up by now or not?

Kasturi: I don't know. *(sees him sleeping)*

There he is. Keep sleeping man, sleep.

(Enters the hut. After sometime, comes out of the hut, and hangs up the wet saree on the bamboo bar to dry. While stroking her wet long hair to dry, she noticed that Asim was slyly peeping at her.)

Kasturi: (*gets furious*) Ahh!

Hello, hey!

You stranger! What are you peeping at?

Don't you have any shame?

Asim: (*takes out his face from the covered blanket, smiles and sings*)

Having seen your face as the Sun rises, I will have a good day.

Kasturi: Get up! Get lost from here.

Do you think this is an almshouse?

All such fair-skinned strangers these days! They might look neat, tidy and well off but are actually bloody thieves, beggars or tramps.

Get out of here! Get up, I said! You bloody nasty, wretched rascal.

Look at you, peeping and smiling at unknown girls!

Asim: (*stands up*) Oh! Why do I have to face such vile accusations?

I didn't say anything to you.

Kasturi: Didn't say anything? Want to see how I will gouge your eyes out?

Asim: Is there anything wrong in seeing you?

'If it soothes the eyes, why not see it?'

Kasturi: Bring the stick, Phula.

I will hit this rascal and kick him out.

Asim: Why do you get so furious?

Kasturi: If you wish for your well-being, then leave immediately.

Asim: What will you do if I don't move?

Kasturi: What can I do? I will sweat you out with my beatings.

Asim: (*laughs*) Oh! Sweating me out will be so nice of you!

Kasturi: Where are you from, shameless fellow?

Asim: I am from this place.

Kasturi: Had you been from here, won't we have recognized you?

Asim: You can, if you are willing to recognize.
But you hiss at me.

Maharagu: (*coming from the village*) Where has this fellow dropped from?

Kasturi: Dada, look at this shameless fellow.

Maharagu: Haebo! Watch out (*rushes to him*)
I will wring your neck out and throw it away.

Asim: Why would you do that when I have not done anything wrong to you, brother.

Maharagu: You keep staring at an unknown girl!

(*Asim laughs*)

Aentha: (*comes out of the hut*) Nuni, what is this ruckus you are creating early in the morning?

Maharagu: Dada, look at the audacity of this cocky stranger.

Asim: I am not a thief or a destitute.
I am just a human being like you.

Kasturi: Whether a man or a monkey, cast your eyes down like a decent man.

Aentha: If you are done with your bath and morning rituals, go inside. Why are you quarreling here?

Maharagu: Dada, why are you blaming nuni? She is not prattling. This man is a crook.

Aentha: All right! You go and do your work. I will deal with this man.

(*Maharagu leaves, giving Asim a sly leer*)

Asim: I want to wash my face, brother.

Aentha: But will you use water from our house?

Asim: Why not?

Aentha: We are the Bajnia people.
That is why...

Asim: We are all people. Now, what is this Bajnia people?
Bring some water.

Aentha: I will arrange the water, babu.

Hey Phula, bring some water in the brass pot.

Phula: (*inside the hut*) Where did you keep the brass pot, nana?

Kasturi: (*from inside the hut*) Didn't you give it on a mortgage to the wealthy Dina?

Aentha: (*after a pause*) Alright, then bring it in a coconut shell bowl.

(*Phula brings some water on a coconut shell bowl. Asim takes the bowl of water from Aentha, washes his face and then drinks the leftover water.*)

Asim: (*wiping his face*) It is not just water, it is ambrosia.

I had a fire in my belly, which is now cooled.

Aentha: Sit down, babu. (*Asim sits down in the verandah under the eaves*)

What is your name, babu? What do you do? Why have you come here?

Asim: Everyone knows me as Asim. I am a fairly educated man. I am doing research moving across towns, cities, villages and rural areas.

Aentha: What did you say? What do you do?

Asim: Research

Aentha: What is that?

Asim: Research means understanding a matter in great detail.

Aentha: What matter are you researching? Is it a cattle trading fair?

Asim: (*laughs*) More than the cattle. The society we live in comprises of some people who are rich and others who are poor: the haves and the have-nots.

Aentha: True. The haves have surplus and the have-nots starve.

Asim: Since ancient times, in this society, the upper class exploits and the lower class is exploited. This tug of war is because of the conflict between the two classes. Isn't it?

Aentha: Nuni Kasturi, make some tea.

Asim: No need for tea. I had some water.

Kasturi: (*from inside*) There is no sugar at home.
A packet of tea powder is there. Shall I make tea with jaggery?

Aentha: Make it with whatever you can.
If there is no jaggery, then make it with salt.

Asim: (*listens to what Aentha said*)
Some relish the lavish meal, whereas some can't even afford a scrap of salt.

(*Phula runs out of the hut for the village. Kasturi listens to this discussion from the window.*)

Aentha: This is our karma.

What can be done?

Asim: Who says it is your karma?

I am researching on this differentiation in the society, discrimination between the haves and the have-nots. I have a great desire to know more about this issue.

Aentha: What is the point of knowing more about this matter? People say, even the old man 'Gandhi' knew a lot about the issue of poverty and poor people. Has he arrived at any solution to that?

The condition of the poor persists.

Asim: No, no... I don't mean that. The purpose of my research is to understand in depth the age-old traditions, life and culture of such folk musicians in rural areas. I have come to you to know more about the folk songs, folk music, folk plays, local music, traditional folk musical instruments, instrumentalists, pastorale, local hymns, traditional ballads, melodies, warbles, sacred songs in rural areas, tunes, lyrics and also the folk music like 'Rasarkeli' and 'Dalkhai.' I also want to explore the possibilities of its progress and carry it forward for future generations.

Aentha: We don't have any of these. We are Bajnias, the instrumentalists. We play traditional folk musical instruments, Dhol-Nisan-Tasa-Jhanj-Muhuri, to reproduce a tune, melody, piece of music or note on an instrument, on call on certain occasions and gatherings to earn our living. I wonder, what is that you will get out of this?

Asim: There is a lot that I can seek from this, brother. After perceiving, understanding and learning these things, I will write a great book on them. Your names and pictures will be printed on it and many will know you. The entire nation will come across your names.

Aentha: We are frogs of the well. What will you achieve by taking us to the seas? Are we mentioned in any books or scripts? We are insignificant like the pebbles of the farm. What will you achieve by writing about us in your book? Why don't you take the assistance of big people? We small people can't be of much use for anyone. There is a common saying – 'sitting under a huge evergreen tree can at least give you shade, what can you get sitting under a bare tree?'

Asim: I am in search of bare trees that don't give shade. I don't have anything to do with huge evergreen trees. I am a 'Bhukha' and I am in search of all the Bhukhas like me in this society. I want to understand and get a feel of their customs and culture, life and living, happiness and sorrows. What can be done so that we can all become one? And can live our lives by sharing with each other? No one will have surplus and no one will have less.

Aentha: This is an awkward concept that you are talking about babu.

Asim: It is not an awkward concept, even if it seems awkward to you.

Aentha: Since Dina has a lot of wealth, does that mean he will share all his property with us?

Has it happened ever anywhere?

Asim: Why should we think that it will not happen, since it has not happened yet?

Aentha: I don't think this is possible.

Asim: We can't just think that this will happen, we need to make it happen and prove it.

Aentha: This is beyond my understanding.

Asim: My research is on the poor, wretched, deprived, underprivileged and backward people of the society.

Aentha: What can we do?

Asim: You can do everything, brother. I enquired a lot about you and then finally reached you after asking many people from nearby.

Aentha: Listen, babu! If you can, then fight. We are like half-dead snakes. None of us can raise our hoods, or hiss and bite.

Asim: This requires mental willpower and physical strength.

Aentha: Hey girl, how long will you take to boil the tea?

Kasturi: (*from inside*) I have sent Phula to Dina's shop.

Aentha: I told you to make tea with jaggery and you still sent her to Dina's?

We are already deep in Dina's debt. I wonder if he can give us more on top of that!

Kasturi: (*from inside*) I am sure he will, that is why I have sent her.

Aentha: That day when I met him, he pestered me a lot to settle my accounts with him.

Asim: Has your work and income been knocked down?

Aentha: Did you say knocked down?

It will be even more difficult to survive this year.

Asim: Is your musical group not getting business?

Aentha: Listen, babu!

This year we didn't get rain at all. There is a drought everywhere. Farmlands have almost become scorched. People having any money whatsoever call us for music and entertainment. Money results in welfare.

But those having even a little money, want modern music. Why will they ask for our archaic music? I wonder.

Asim: (*laughs*) Modern music.

(*Phula returns home with empty hands. With a gloomy face, she enters the hut and speaks to her aunt whimpering.*)

Phula: The wealthy Dina did not give anything, nana.

Kasturi: He didn't? How much can he give on credit?

Phula: (*weeps*) I won't go to his shop anymore.
I won't nana.
He threatened me and threw me out of the shop.
I won't go again, aunt.

Aentha: (*hears everything*) Did you just say that Dina threw you out?
Does he have that kind of audacity?
Bring my Muhuri, I will go to him and see why he didn't give you groceries.

Kasturi: (*inside the hut*) Phula, take this Muhuri and give it to your father.

(*Phula gives the Muhuri to Aentha*)

Aentha: (*grabs the Muhuri from Phula and holds it adoringly and whimpers*)
Please wait, babu. I will be back.

(*while leaving, he sees Dina arriving*)

Dina: How many Muhuris do you have dada to put on mortgage and buy things?

How can I keep lending endlessly?

Aentha: Our Phula had been to your shop.

You sent her back empty-handed, isn't it?

Dina: First, clear your previous dues and then you can buy whatever you want.

Aentha: I have a new guest at home, and I wanted to offer him some tea. How could you refuse to give things? Take my Muhuri and keep it as a mortgage. In return, give me two kilos of rice, tea powder, sugar, potato and pulses. My nuni will go and get it from you.

Dina: Whether a guest is new or old, items for sale are always new. Remember this! You can buy things only with hard cash, not just talks.

Aentha: Dada, what did you say?

Dina: What else can I say?

First, pay me the outstanding and then send nuni to get things.

Aentha: But I am asking you to keep the Muhuri.

Dina: What will I do with the Muhuri?

Can I eat it? I want money. You know it well. It's all about money.

Aentha: If I had the money, why would I have offered you my Muhuri? This Muhuri is everything to me: my father, my mother, my god. Do you understand that?

Dina: Oh! If this Muhuri is your god, then why are you all in extreme poverty? Listen, I am telling you, pay me the outstanding money and then take new items. Leave this farce. Don't give me an attitude.

What kind of people are you all? You have taken so much on credit. Someday, at least you should pay back a bit of that money. My shop can't be running like this. Where were all these rascals? In what god-damned moment did I set up this shop? It seems all of you have come together to devastate me. I am a socially conscious man. I am succour to everyone here. So many hungry mouths to feed. How much can I take care of? Go die, you ungrateful wretches!

(*Dina leaves. Asim is looking through his research papers. In the meanwhile, Kasturi comes out of the hut with a bowl of tea. Seeing this...*)

Aentha: Did you see that, learned babu? This is our plight. This is how we live our life with ups and down. (*looks at Kasturi*) Listen, nuni, you give tea to our learned babu. I am going to Gahadu's house. I will be back soon, you be seated.

(*goes towards the village*)

(*Kasturi keeps the bowl of tea on the verandah and stands in a corner. Asim starts sipping the tea.*)

Asim: Did you make the tea with salt?

Kasturi: Do you think we are so inferior?

Asim: I didn't think so. I am just asking?

Kasturi: (*blushes coyly*) I made it with sugar!

Asim: Tea prepared by you will taste sugary even if you had put salt!

Kasturi: (*coyly*) You are such a flirt!

Asim: No, I am nothing much, just a common and a poor man like all of us here.

Kasturi: (*smiles*) Will you stay here for long?

Asim: (*smiles*) Ibua! But a moment ago you were kicking me out from here!

Kasturi: I thought you were a stranger, not from here.

Asim: Then why a change of mind?

Kasturi: After listening to your sweet talks.

Asim: (*teases*) What's up in your mind?

Kasturi: (*smiles*)

Asim: I have lots of work to do, I need to go to many villages.

Kasturi: What do you do in all those villages?

Asim: I keep calculating and do accounts.

Kasturi: Of what?

Asim: Of girls!

Kasturi: (*smiles*) What! Liar!

Asim: This is what happens these days.
If you tell the truth, they will call you liar
If you tell them a lie...

Kasturi: They will call you truthful...
Now I know the attributes of this truthful man.
(*loudly*) Hey Phula!

Phula: (*from inside*) Hmm.

Kasturi: Come to me, I will comb your hair.

Phula: (*from inside*) Coming.

(*Phula comes with a wooden comb. Kasturi makes her sit on the verandah, and combs her hair while catching louse from Phula's hair. In between, she keeps looking at Asim. Even Asim is busy writing something in his diary and keeps looking at Kasturi, smiling. When they make proper eye contact with each other, a faint song is heard from inside the hut.*)

Song: Boy: How can I forget you?
My life is colourful with you.
Filled with so many colours of the spring
The fresh fragrance of the young buds spreading
With the lovely breeze blowing.

Girl: (*following the same tune*)

You and me...

(*Kasturi whispers something into Phula's ears. Later Phula tells Asim*)

Phula: Haego, what do you like to eat? My nana is asking.

Asim: (*closes the diary*) Ummm...

Are you asking me, nuni?

I'd like your nana to make Arsa pitha coated with lots of sesame seeds and clarified butter.

Kasturi: (*listens to his reply*)

You can ask me to bake sweets like Kanda Phulki and Dudra out of wild fruits and leaves. How can we afford Arsa Pitha?

Asim: Alright! Alright!

You said it right, nuni. Why should you make Arsa pitha? In fact, these days butter and oil are adulterated, you know that.

Phula: (*after a while*) Then what do you suggest?

Asim: If you insist,

tell your nana,

I can like even a slice of simple salty roasted rice cake

(*looks at Kasturi*)

I love the crunchy crust of the cake...

Phula: (*comes to Kasturi*)

Nana, he loves the crunchy crab.

(*Hearing Phula confusing 'crust' with 'crab' both Asim and Kasturi laugh. Once again, a song is heard from inside the hut...*)

Song: Girl: You are the caramelized butter and sesame seeds coated sweet Arsa Pitha of my thatched house

Boy: Whoosh! Whoosh! Squally rain

showers of the dark dense clouds.

You are the precious stack of Jhilliparagi paddy panicle of my threshing yard.

Both: You and me...

Boy: You are the sparkling star of my sleepy innocent eyes,

twinkling in my night's dreams

Girl: You are the pristine water, red rosary pea,

my pure silver nose pin.

I will keep you as a rainbow in the clear sky.

Both: You and me...

(*During this song, Asim's and Kasturi's mutual attraction and developing love are seen. Both come home walking through the pond and mango grove. Kasturi serves food to Asim. Kasturi sits next to him and smiles shyly as Asim starts to eat the food. Day and night settings have also been projected.)*

(*Now the scene is back to its original form – Kasturi combing Phula's hair. At the end of the song, Kasturi and Asim gaze into each other's eyes. While combing unknowingly Kasturi pulls Phula's hair a bit hard. Phula shouts.*)

Phula: Oh! It's hurting, nana...

(*Hearing her, Kasturi and Asim wake up from their fantasy and laugh shyly.*)

Complete darkness on the stage.

Scene III

(*Dusk arrives rapidly. Aentha is sitting on the verandah, coughing. Ribs and spine are visible on his skinny body.*)

Aentha: Nuni Kasturi.
Where did this girl go?
She is a little too outgoing, girl!

Phula: (*comes out of the house*) Are you asking for something, father?

Aentha: Nothing much, dear.
Please bring my Muhuri.

(*Phula brings the Muhuri from home and gives it to Aentha.*)

Aentha: Where did your nana go, nuni?

Phula: She said that she is going out to purchase a few things.

Aentha: Did she go to Dina's shop?

Phula: Maybe. When I insisted on going with her, she rebuked me.

She said, 'Why would you go out in the middle of the night? With all the snakes and insects around.'

Aentha: (*smiles*) She said right, dear. You are a child.

Phula: She told me that she will bring peppermint candy and yellow pipe crunch rolls for me.

Aentha: Oh, really! Please share one with me, dear.

Phula: No... I won't give it to anyone.

I will eat alone.

Yellow pipe crunch rolls taste so good, isn't it father?

Aentha: Yes daughter, they taste good.

You go and play for now. Come home when your nana is back.

Phula: Father, nana was telling me that the festival Puspuni is coming.

Aentha: Yes, dear.

It will come this year too, like every year.

Phula: You have to buy me a new frock this Puspuni, father.

Aentha: (*to himself*) Well, if I get some money, only then we can buy one.

Phula: Look father, this frock is torn.

Nana stitched it, but it tore again at the same place, like a wide-open mouth.

Aentha: (*cuddles Phula*) Dear, everything for us is going to be a hungry wide-open mouth.

Phula: Which variety of pitha will we have this Puspuni, father?

Aentha: We will make all varieties of sweets: pupchi, sualin, dudra, arsa.

Phula: Manda pitha?

Aentha: Yes. Manda pitha, too. We will make so many other types too.

Phula: I know how to make manda pitha, father. We make round balls to make manda pitha, isn't it, father?

Aentha: Your nana will teach you dear. Go and see whether your nana is back or not.

Phula: (*claps seeing Kasturi arriving*) Hey father!
Nana is back.
She brought me yellow crunch pipe rolls.
She brought me peppermint candies.
My nana is back.

(*Kasturi returns after the shopping. Phula hugs her.*)

Haego nana, give me the crunch rolls.

Kasturi: Come inside, I will give you.

Phula: No, give it to me here.

Kasturi: Take it then! (*takes out a packet of crunch rolls and gives it to Phula*)

Phula: (*Eats and shows it to Aentha to tempt him)* Hey father... nah... nah... (*smiling, Phula enters the home*)

Aentha: Did you bring everything, nuni?

Kasturi: Got a few things only, though he was reluctant to give them too.

Aentha: Did Mahajan say anything?

Kasturi: No, he didn't say anything.

Aentha: There is not much that even he can do.

After all, how much can he give on credit?

It is because of his mercy that this jaw is functioning and this hungry mouth is fed.

Kasturi: I got few things for Puspuni. I will get the rest of the things later.

Aentha: What celebration of Puspuni this year, dear?

People didn't even perform the rites in their farmlands on the eve of the harvest.

The lands are so barren because of the drought.

Kasturi: But can festivals and celebrations be ignored?

Aentha: They can celebrate only if they have some resources.

Kasturi: With or without resources, people will celebrate.

Aentha: Every year during Puspuni, our troupe never gets any free time. This year, there is not even a single call, my dear. There is no fascination even for Puspuni like before. For Puspuni, people used to get excited from fifteen days before.

It was celebrated throughout the year.

Goddess Lakshmi comes to the house from the farmland. My grandfather used to talk about the coronation of kings. People offered green beans, black matpe, pigeon peas, and sesame seeds from their crops. The king even joyously provided a feast of rice and goat curry to the people. Gave them some money for drinks as well. Our troupes were not free for days, nights or even for a few moments – either we would go to get chher-chhera from door-to-door, or play music in front of the king's palace, or at the Gauda's area, or with the stilt walking performers. Always busy performing!

Kasturi: These days those customs are not celebrated anymore anywhere.

People cook some dishes and sweets in their houses, and the drunkards create a ruckus after having a few drinks.

Aentha: Is the same old traditional system maintained these days?

What shall I tell you, nuni?
You were a kid, younger than our Phula,
I was going out to people's doors to get chherchhera, you were adamant on going with me.
You started shouting to go with me.
What else could I have done?
So, I took you along with me.
I carried you on my shoulder.
You were just a toddler... How could you have walked such a long distance?

Kasturi: (*startled*) Me?

Aentha: See... you don't trust me?
Yes, you... (*laughs*)
I went around carrying you on my shoulder.
There was a village headman at that time, the moment he saw you, he told me –
'Haebo, Aentha,
Which family does this girl belong to?
She is so cute, chubby and extremely beautiful!'
I saluted him and said,
'Gauntia Huzoor! She is my sister.'
Gauntia was startled and said,
'Huh...Is she your sister? Keep it in mind Aentha, I am telling you from a conservative family holding thirty-two core principles, she is a lady

of quality holding thirty-two core qualities. She is a fortunate girl.' (*smiles happily*)

Sometimes I still recall the words of the Gauntia.

During the festival of Puspuni, there used to be so much to eat, to drink, so much music – if you asked for chher-chhera, they spewed out huge amount of paddy rice into our bags.

But these days, if you ask them, they are reluctant to give.

Kasturi: People will offer you paddy rice and call you to play music, only if they have something to offer.

Aentha: Even if they call us to perform, how can we?

Maharagu was talking about giving his Dhol on a mortgage.

If the troupe keeps on giving everything on mortgage, how will we play music and celebrate Puspuni?

Kasturi: What can we do dada?

On the eve of Puspuni, our mind is so elated, can't wrap my mind around it.

The mind desires to wear a new saree.

I had an old Saptapar saree of my deceased sister-in-law, I wore it for two years and now it is torn at several places. Despite so much of stitching and patching up, it won't last anymore.

We don't have a fortune dada, god chose us to be born into poverty. We need only a handful to eat and a piece of clothing, and we can't seem to muster even that. The mind is melancholic and the heart heavy.

I feel like sitting in a corner of the house behind closed doors and cry my heart out.

(*her eyes flood with tears*)

Leave it, it is our karma.

Aentha: (*changes the topic*) Did you bring the packet of bidi for me?

Kasturi: Stop smoking dada, didn't the doctor advise you that day?

Aentha: What does the doctor know about me, nuni?

In fact, this bidi is everything for me.

After Phula's mother passed away, this bidi kept me alive.

Kasturi: What do you mean kept you alive?

This bidi will take away your life. (*leaves*)

Aentha: Nuni, where did that learned babu go?

He is not back yet.

Kasturi: Must be coming back.

He was talking about going to Hadu's home.

Aentha: He is a nice boy.

He might be from a well-off family, but he can sacrifice his life for the betterment of the poor and the destitute.

Kasturi: What does he do?

Keeps reading and writing the whole night!

Aentha: He is doing a great lot of work for us. If he is successful, then our situation will change perhaps.

Kasturi: These kinds of people say many good things, but who knows how much of this fructifies?

Aentha: He doesn't seem to be a liar. He is a genuinely nice boy. He told me something.

Kasturi: What did he say, dada?

Aentha: Leave it, I will tell you later.

Kasturi: Why later? Tell me now, please.

Aentha: He said that he loves you.

Kasturi: Why shouldn't he love me?

Aentha: It is not like that, girl.

Kasturi: Then what is it like?

After all, I cooked and served him food, and he ate to his satisfaction.

Why shouldn't he love me?

Aentha: That is what you think.

Kasturi: Everyone behaves well in their time of need, and once they have extracted what they want out of you, they show their true colours and don't care anymore.

Aentha: (*breathes heavily*)

He is a nice person...

Nobody can predict anybody's destiny.

(*Asim sir arrives. Kasturi was about to tell him something, but gets shy and goes back to the house.*)

Aentha: Come, learned babu, we were talking about you.

Asim: A discussion on me! I hope I haven't committed a mistake unknowingly?

Aentha: Is it that we discuss someone only when he has committed a mistake?

Asim: My work in this village is almost over.

Aentha: I see. You completed it very soon, it seems.

Asim: Yes, it has been a long time since I came here. I have interacted with everyone, understood them, taken everyone's interview and documented it.

Aentha: What will you do next?

(*Kasturi listens to them from the window*)

Asim: I will write my thesis on it and submit it to the government. After it is passed and accepted by the government, I may get a decent job.

Aentha: You will get a nice job.

Asim: Even I hope for a nice job.

Aentha: Will you remember us once you get a job, brother?

Asim: Come on, no way can I forget you, that is not possible.

I give you my word, Muhuria dada, I will be back after I get the job.

Aentha: (*holds Asim's hand*)

I am not bothered... if anything were to happen to me... if you accept Kasturi, I will be relieved from a great burden.

Asim: Why a great burden? She is such an adorable girl. If god wishes, he will fulfil all your wishes.

Aentha: You don't know anything about me, learned babu. Kasturi is my only sister.

My mother died after giving birth to her.

I have raised her as my daughter.

I will be relieved of this burden after I get her married and send her to her in-law's house.

Asim: You don't worry at all.

Aentha: Sometimes, the mind doesn't get convinced.

You are from a well-off family, upper caste.

Whether you will like and accept low people like us... I am not sure.

Asim: It is not like that brother, what shall I tell you about me?

Even I am from a poor family. I have never known or seen my parents since birth. I am a self-made man. I don't believe in and accept this caste system, brother.

I just understand humanity.

Humanity is everything.

Humanity is my caste.

Humanity is my mother and father.

Humanity is my everything.

Aentha: Saying is different from doing.

Asim: I know.

I understand.

Something is disturbing your mind that is why you don't understand what I say.

Aentha: I understand, babu.

Asim: Then what else are you thinking?

Aentha: I understand, babu.

But she was born a girl... not a brass pot or tumbler that I can exchange.

She is a clay pot, if broken once, her whole life will be wasted. (*weeps*)

Asim: (*embraces Aentha...*)

Don't think I am such a worthless man, Muhuria dada...

Keeping the Guardians of Directions as my witness, I promise you today, there is no difference between Kasturi and me...

I will marry her, brother.

What more can I say?

Aentha: (*falls at Asim's feet...*)

It is done brother, Kasturi is yours now.

She is the glittering star of my eyes, but now onwards, she is yours.

(*starts coughing... coughs heavily... faints bleeding from his mouth*)

Asim: (*makes Aentha sit in the verandah and shouts*)

Kasturi!

Bring some water!

Kasturi: (*from inside the house*) Why? What happened?

Asim: Nothing has happened.

Just bring some water!

Aentha: From where did I get this blood in my mouth, learned babu?

Kasturi: (*holding water*) Imaa!

My brother is bleeding from his mouth.

What happened to my brother?

Come inside and sleep for a while, take some rest.

Asim: Kasturi, hold brother Aentha, we will take him inside the house.

(*Asim and Kasturi take him inside the house. While coming out of the house...*)

Asim: Don't be worried!

Kasturi: Why? What has happened?

Asim: Brother Aentha started bleeding from his mouth while coughing.

Kasturi: Did he fall and hurt himself?

Asim: You are stupid... blood was oozing out from his mouth.

Kasturi: Yes, I saw that... blood oozing out.

Asim: Do you know what happens when someone coughs out blood?

Kasturi: What happens?

Asim: T.B...

Kasturi: What is that?

Asim: That is a disease.

Kasturi: Will he be cured?

Asim: He can be cured but he has to take medication.

Kasturi: Imaa!
What shall I do now?

Will my dada be cured or not?

Asim: People say the liver gets diseased in such cases.

Kasturi: If the liver gets diseased, how will the person survive?

Asim: Different kinds of medicines are available these days. He will be cured, don't worry.

Kasturi: I am very much in a panic.

What will happen to my brother...?

My body is getting cold because of nervousness.

My hands and legs are trembling and my head is spinning.

(*She sits down out of nervousness.*)

Asim: Why are you so nervous?

I am with you. Don't worry.

Kasturi: I see darkness everywhere.

If anything, unfortunately, were to happen to my brother, how would I live?

The very thought drowns me in misery. (*screams softly*)

Asim: Why do you scream? Brother Muhuria should not get to know that he has T.B.

If he comes to know about this, he will be shattered and despondent.

Kasturi: How long can we hide this matter from him?

How long can you hide a cub in a haystack?

Asim: No matter how long it may be, but we have to take care of dada.

Kasturi: You are with us at this moment, but for how long.

Asim: I will come back, even if I have to go now.

Kasturi: Long distance friendship is like hay fire, which dies out soon. How can you trust them?

Asim: Please have faith in me, Kasturi.

Once my research is over, I will submit my papers to the government.

Kasturi: Then you will get a great job and too much money. Will you care anymore for us, poor destitute people?

We are wretched people. Nobody stands with us.

You know that, poor people are considered the enemies of the country. If you had not come to this village, would such great research work have ever been possible?

Although you are high born, you interacted and socialized with people like us. You ate with us. You became one with us, in both good and bad times.

Even I have devoted my soul to you. Since you were here, time passed surprisingly quickly. I could listen to all your sweet talks. I used to serve you food and you would eat it happily. You pampered Phula!

Asim: (*sits close to Kasturi*) Kasturi!

Kasturi: We spent so much time together, talking to each other in the mango grove...

We couldn't even realize the moonrise and moonset of the nights...

Asim: Kasturi!

Kasturi: Were those lovely moments?

How will I live this life alone without you?

Tell me, dear!

How will my brother get well?

If you don't come back to me, I will be shattered.

I don't have any other support!

(*starts crying*)

Asim: (*hugs Kasturi*)

I am giving you my word, Kasturi.

Whether I get a job or not, I will come back to you for sure.

I am not that great a man as you think, Kasturi.

I am just a normal human being like all of us here.

Kasturi, I swear on you, I swear on myself, I swear on anybody you say I will come back to you, surely.

I will put vermillion on your forehead and bangles on your hands and I will marry you.

Kasturi: I am trembling with a sudden fear...

Asim: Why are you tense Kasturi?

Kasturi: You know my plight!

My brother is sick.

My niece is a small child.

We don't even have a handful to eat.

Asim: Everything will be alright...

Kasturi: Because of the drought this year food is scarce everywhere.

People will die like insects and worms out of poverty. Peasants could not even get a little paddy.

Asim: Our country doesn't have any scarcity, Kasturi. There is corruption in the whole process, starting from the distribution of public goods and services from the Centre till it reaches the common men.

There is a drought in this place, but in other parts of the country, there is surplus.

The government will positively bring goods from those areas and provide to people in this part.

Kasturi: Not only paddy but people are also beggared for fuelwood.

The government may provide in some time, but at this time people are in starvation.

(*Aentha coughs from inside the house*)

Asim: Kasturi, please go inside and check what happened to Aentha dada?

Kasturi: Imaa!

What happened to my dada?

Dada, oh dada!

Aentha: (*from inside the house*)

Nuni, please give me some water.

(*Kasturi enters the house. Maharagu arrives with the Dhol slung around his shoulder.*)

Maharagu: (*puts down the Dhol*) Hey, learned babu, I heard from people that you are leaving today?

Asim: I have to leave today.

Maharagu: Can't you leave after Puspuni?

Asim: It is all about timing, Dhulia dada.

I have to submit all my research papers as per the stipulated time, and then my work is over.

Maharagu: You would call me a flatterer, if I say it straight to your face, and you would term me sly if I said it behind your back but the truth is, I have never seen a person as nice as you.

Asim: I am not god.

Neither am I so special.

There are much better people than me.

Maharagu: Really, I am not able to understand or believe this, learned babu.

You opened our eyes.

We were living a desolate life, like scattered fieldstones in a pasture.

Exposed to the flaming sun, storms and piercing cold, poverty and hard times had almost crippled our spine.

We were ignorant of our force, strength and power.

You made us aware and realize that even we, who were lying like lifeless stones, have a life.

You gave us a new life.

We need a person like you.

You are like our God Ramachandra!

Asim: Dhulia dada, I understand your mental state, the age-old heart-rending memories of your struggle against poverty and pain.

My research, my devotion, my diligence is solely for people like you.

The purpose of my visit to this village was to serve you all.

You might not know this, Dhulia dada, but your dance, songs, Dhol and all musical instruments that you play, is of great value to me.

Never expect anything from other people.

They will only mock you.

To crucify the self to save mankind is not so easy, Dhulia dada.

I know, nobody has done anything for you people yet and won't even do.

But have faith in me.

My identity may be lost in the crowd.

I may lose my happiness.

Even if they blame me as a culprit or a sinner and punish me in the higher courts of law, or hang me till death, but I will give you your position in this society as human beings.

My book on you will be published, your names along with your photos will be printed in it.

Someday, you will become great people, with your head held high in this society.

Just keep me in your prayers, brother, so that I succeed in this work.

Maharagu: You will surely succeed.

Honestly, if ten more people like you come forward, the world will change completely and become a better place.

Asim: I am leaving, Dhulia dada.

Please call Gahadu, Paltu and Hadu dada so that I can meet them once before leaving.

(*Meanwhile Gahadu, Paltu and Hadu arrive carrying their musical instruments.*)

Maharagu: Hey, we were just talking about them and they arrived...

You will live a long life. Where have you all been?

Hadu: One of Dharni's folks died.

We returned now, after doing the cleaning work there.

Maharagu: The learned babu is leaving today.

Paltu: (*putting his instrument down*)

Really! Learned babu.

Are you leaving today?

(*Coughing sound comes from inside the house. Kasturi comes out of the house and stands in the verandah.*)

Asim: I don't feel like leaving you people.

But I have to do something for this hungry stomach.

I have to go now but I will come back!

Gahadu: Will you come back, babu?

Asim: I will surely come back.
How can I forget the melody of your musical instruments?
Do you think that I can ever forget the euphony of your music and songs?
Aentha dada is unwell, please take care of him until I come back.

Hadu: Its true, learned babu.
Those memorable days that you stayed and spent with us, you charmed us with your mantra and tactic.
You mixed and bonded.
You blended with us like water and milk.

(*Phula walks towards Asim*)

Phula: When will you come back?

Asim: I will come back.
How can I live without you, nuni?

Phula: What will you bring for me?

Asim: You tell me, what shall I bring for you?

Phula: Bring me a balloon.

(*Asim holds Phula in his arms and takes her to Kasturi.*)

Asim: I will bring it dear. I will bring big balloons for our nuni to play with.

(*calls*) Aentha dada! (*Aentha cames*)

I am leaving, dada.

Aentha: Go, learned babu.

May God bless you with success.

(*Kasturi brings some water filled in a coconut shell bowl and keeps it at Asim's feet, a gesture of auspiciousness.*)

Please write letters to us, babu.

Asim: Yes, I will write and send letters.

I am leaving brothers.

(*Asim greets everyone with folded hands, hangs his cotton sling bag on his shoulder and while leaving, turns back and looks at Kasturi. A song hums from inside the house* How can I forget you... *Asim leaves. Kasturi, unable to hold her emotions anymore, goes inside the house.*)

Aentha: Hey boys, did you see it?

How our Kasturi feels shattered?

We were all so happy because of the presence of the learned babu.

Maharagu: Learned babu had become a part of our lives.

Even we are totally disheartened.

We feel forlorn!

Let's play some music.

It will ease our minds at least.

Hadu: Mind doesn't feel like playing music today.
I feel as if my hands are tied up.

Maharagu: Haebo Paltu, hold the Nisan and play.

Paltu: I am not sure whether my drumsticks can even play today.

Maharagu: Hold the sticks, hold it.
We need to ease our minds by playing music.

Hadu: Pick up your Dhol, Maharagu.
Since dada says, hold your instrument.

(*Everyone picks up their instruments and starts playing. Aentha brings his Muhuri from inside to play and in the meanwhile, wealthy Dina arrives.*)

Dina: Haebo rascals!
You are having fun here, aren't you?
Here you are frolicking with your music, and there I am unable to sustain my shop? Is it that you want to see me end up shutting my shop.
Haebo Hadu, do you even keep an account of the payments that you owe me?
You paupers, how much can I give you on credit?
You buy on credit, but don't pay a single penny for it. And I just keep on noting it in your account books.
What good is that account book, if at the end of the day you don't square your accounts?

You are relishing the food on credit, aren't you?

Now, either you pay it today, or I won't allow you to live in this village.

Let's have a scuffle today and let's settle it once and for all.

Don't you know me?

I am the wealthy Dina.

I am being nice to you, but, if I lose my temper, I will make your life very difficult.

You paupers, you bloody starved rascals, either you pay me the outstanding sum right now or you will give me all your personal belongings.

I will auction off your lands and houses, do you know that?

I will beat you black and blue, do you hear me?

Have you forgotten the beating you have had in the past?

What do you think I am? You have taken me for granted.

Whenever you come to my shop to buy goods, you impatient rascals, you start growling and glare at me with angry red fierce eyes if you aren't attended to immediately.

Haebo Aentha, do you remember when you had a guest at your home?

You had sent your nuni to my shop to get things.

When I returned her empty-handed, you gave me attitude.

Now, when I ask for money, you start sweating?

Bring out all your belongings, whatever you have at home.

(*Aentha listens to him, then looks at everyone with sad eyes, everyone is disheartened. Aentha takes the Dhol from Maharagu, Tasa from Hadu, Nisan from Paltu, Jhanj from Gahadu, and his own Muhuri and keeps it in front of Dina, folds his hands and says...*)

Aentha: Wealthy brother, this is all yours.

This is all we have, and this is everything for us.

These musical instruments, whatever we have, take all these away.

If you want to kick us out from this place, then do that.

We won't object.

Every dog has his day, brother. What goes around, comes around.

Today, you can rebuke us, abuse us, and we will bear it stoically.

But brother, try to recall the past, what is there that we have not done for you?

At your wedding, we played music all day and night.

You had guests from Raipur. Don't you remember how much they praised our music?

You, upper class people are ungrateful and forget things quickly.

Ask this Maharagu, when your wife was unable to deliver the baby, how much he did for you?

And today you are treating us like worthless pebbles.

This life has borne all the pains, wealthy brother. What more shall I tell you?

We have stood by you at all times and in all your problems.

We ploughed your field with bullocks when you didn't have ploughmen.

We thrashed your rotting paddy in your thrashing field when you didn't have enough labour.

My father worked his entire life for you, and became hunchbacked with the severe workload, and finally died while working for you.

My father died, my mother died and even my wife died in front of you.

This life has borne all the tortures of fate.

But, this torture from you right now is the extreme.

(*cries*)

Do whatever you want.
Haebo Hadu, what are you looking at?
Let's go, we will all leave this village.
Brother Dina gets all our houses.
Let him auction it, sell it, or even donate it.
Everything belongs to him now.
Nuni Kasturi, come out, bring Phula with you.
Let's leave this place, boys.

Phula: (*comes out of the house*) Where will we go, father?

Aentha: It is such a big world, we will go somewhere.
Everything belongs to the wealthy brother now.
He is kicking us out of this place.

Phula: I won't go, I won't go, dear father. I will not go anywhere leaving our house behind.

(*she goes ranting*)

Aentha: (*angrily*)
You won't go?
You are such a small child and you are shouting that you don't want to go?

(*Aentha beats Phula hard. Kasturi runs to her. Everyone tries to stop him from beating Phula but Aentha keeps beating her. Phula keeps blabbering. Dina, unable to tolerate it anymore, pulls Phula away from him.*)

Dina: Are you a human being or a monkey?

Aentha: Yes... Yes... I am a monkey.

Dina: The child will die from your beatings.
Do you want to kill her?

Phula: I will not go anywhere else, I will stay here only, dear father.

Dina: Yes, my dear, you will live here only.
Nobody will kick you out from here.

Hadu: Wealthy dada!

Dina: (*to Kasturi*)
Hey dear, take Phula, wash her face.

(*Kasturi takes away Phula from him*)

Maharagu, pick up your Dhol. Get up, all of you. Take your instruments.

(*No one listens to him. He asks them loudly*)

Rascals, come here and take your instruments.

(*Everyone takes away their instruments and sits down*)

Now play some music.

(*No one listens to him. Again, he tells loudly*)

Hey you rascals, play the music.

(*Everyone looks at Aentha*)

Aentha dada, why this sullen face now? Pick up your Muhuri, blow it tight. Hey boys, you didn't get to know well your wealthy Dina yet? I am

not a traitor, I told you that I will kick you out, but will I really kick you out?
Play music, you rascals

(*Picks up the Muhuri and hands it over to Aentha.*)

Aentha dada...

Aentha: (*Looks at Dina for a while, then takes the Muhuri*)
Haebo Hadu, pick up your instrument.
Haebo Paltu, pick up your Nisan.
Our master is insisting. Play it once

(*everyone plays music together*)

Dina: (*after he listens to the music*)
Now I feel somewhat happy.
Keep your instruments with you.
This year we will celebrate Puspuni in a grand way, understood?
Hadu... what groceries do you want for Puspuni?
Gahadu?

Gahadu: Yes?

Dina: How many pegs will you drink boy?
Well, I am the wealthy Dina!
I can never forget your favours.
Just that I spoke bit harshly to you out of anger, and you all became sullen faced.
Don't you know?

I am one of you.

If you die, I will die with you.

Wherever you go, I will go with you.

Just because I spoke a few harsh words, all of you were ready to move out...?

Aentha dada... how can I live without you...?

Ahhh! I may lose the wealth, but my mind is twined with you.

(*started weeping*)

Aentha: Haebo master... don't even we make mistakes?

Please forgive us, master.

Maharagu: Yes, master.

Don't even we have faults?

You should not hold onto such things.

Dina: But see.

Prepare well for Puspuni.

And whatever you want for it, buy it from my shop.

My shop is always open for all of you, I am not such a starved person.

Hadu: Yes master.

(*bows his head to him, falls at his feet*)

Where else shall we go other than your shop, master?

Do we have any other option?
Isn't it boys?

Dina: Dear Phula, come with me.
I will give you crunch rolls and fried snacks.

Phula: (*goes to Aentha*)
Shall I go, father?
I am fond of crunch rolls and fried snacks.

Maharagu: Hey Aentha dada, let nuni go with him.
She has insisted many times on going.

Phula: Shall I go, father?

Aentha: (*caresses her head*)
Go dear... go with your wealthy dada.

(*Dina leaves carrying Phula with him*)

This is a very awkward situation... (*after a beat*)
Hey Hadu, who will play another pair of Nisan on Puspuni?

Hadu: Shall we call the goatherd's eldest son, Hurshi, to play on Puspuni?

Aentha: The goatherd's eldest son?

Hadu: He is from the village Khalia.

Aentha: Yeah, yeah... If he plays well, then what are you waiting for?
You should inform him soon.

Hadu: In that case, I'll leave now?

Aentha: Go, go... (*Hadu leaves*)
Gahadu, Maharagu, Paltu, you also leave, boys. Take your instruments and go.

Everyone: Yes, dada, we are leaving.

Maharagu: let's go... (*after everyone leaves*)

Aentha: (*loudly*) Paltu, stretch and tighten the strings of your instruments properly.

Paltu: (*from a distance*) yes... yes...

Aentha: Yes, just look after it.

(*After everyone leaves, Aentha looks at Kasturi smiling happily.*)

Complete darkness on the stage.

Scene IV

(Early morning, on the day of Puspuni. Once every year, Hadu, Paltu, Gahadu, Maharagu and Hurshi play the music. Hadu sings a song. Everyone sings and dances along with them. Meanwhile, Kasturi plasters the floor of the courtyard with cow dung. She then hangs a sling bag on Phula's shoulder and gives her a stick for chher-cherra. Phula dances off and on.)

Hadu: (*sings*)

Hollow are the bamboo culms
Water of the river Mahanadi swirls
See the cheater mourns.

Wild beads on the trees chiming
Cleanse your eyes and see properly
Our learned babu might be coming.

(*stops singing*)

Hey boys, shall we play some more music... yes... yes. (*resumes singing*)

I constructed mud walls with wet mud lumps
Hey government, will you buy our labour or us?
Either you answer me today
Answer me truly today.

(*While playing music, all of them leave the stage. Aentha arrives coughing through the pond, drunk and asking for chher-chhera at every door of the village.*)

Aentha: My name is Aentha.
Hey, do you hear me?
Hey rascals, you can't even take a stand against me.
I told the contractor's wife, mistress –
Can you give me a small peg?
Scoundrel poured two bottles – I gulped it entirely (*belching*)
Ha...
She gave me 'neat alcohol, vivid red coloured.
My throat got irritated so I ate some snacks. Waah!
How soothing it was!
Contractor's bloody scoundrel wife.
Haebo Hadu, you half dead rogue, if you would have accompanied me, could have had a peg.
Where is my Muhuri?
Dear nuni Kasturi, my wife's sister, my wife...

You scoundrel, keep gobbling food always and garrulous.
Wait... I will send you even, to the hell.
Hey Kasturi, Kas-Kas-and turi, Kass-turi.
You lanky girl, belligerent, dirty runny nose.

Kasturi: (*comes out of the house*)
He is drunk today.
Drunkards don't recognize their mother, sisters and friends even.
Hey, did you drink again?

Aentha: Bloody, who is that?
Who are you to ask me?

(*slaps Kasturi tightly twice*)

Kasturi: (*cries*) You beat me up, brother?
Beat me more...

Aentha: Oh...oh... I beat you up,
Did I beat up my Kasturi?
Did I beat up my lovable Kasturi?

Kasturi: What has happened to you, dada?
Have you lost your mind?

Aentha: Yes... yes... You are right...
My mind is destroyed....
I have become insane. (*laughing*)

(*coughs while laughing*)

Kasturi: Your chest looks strange.
Oh, God!
So much blood is oozing out from your mouth,
What shall I do now?
Where to go?

Aentha: I am bleeding from my mouth, nuni.
Blood... yes, yes... fresh blood,
Hey nuni, this is fresh blood, isn't it?
Bloody, let it flow out.

Kasturi: Dada, come inside and sleep.

Aentha: Hey my dear nuni, I beat you up with this hand, isn't it? Look at this... (*slapped himself*)

Kasturi: Why are you slapping yourself?

Aentha: This hand beat you up, isn't it?
I will cut off this hand and throw it away, do you know that?

Kasturi: Whoever beat me up, maybe.
Your hand didn't beat me up.
What is its fault?

Aentha: Then, whose fault, is it?
Tell me. Otherwise, I will twist your neck.

Kasturi: This alcohol addiction has killed you entirely, dada. It has corroded your liver bit by bit.

Aentha: How will you understand the goodness of this alcohol, nuni?

Kasturi: Goodness, my foot!
Goodness and that too of alcohol...!

Aentha: Drink and make merry!
Haebo Hadu, drink and make merry!

Kasturi: Dada, come inside and sleep.

Aentha: Why should I sleep?
What has happened to me?
Why don't you go and sleep?

Kasturi: (*drags Aentha inside the house*)
Come inside.
Will you come or not?
I will take you to the witch doctor Dharni for treatment.
He can at least try to cure you

Aentha: Alright, let's go.
Whatever you say, wherever you say, I will go.
You are my loveable sister.
Like a mother to me, like a god to me, you are everything to me.

(*Walking towards the village, Kasturi and Aentha moves out of the stage. After sometime, wealthy Dina arrives calling Aentha.*)

Dina: Muhuria dada! Isn't he at home?

(*peeps inside the house*)

He isn't?

(*sees Hadu crossing by*)

Haebo Hadu!

Hadu: Who is that?

Oh, my master... Is it you?

(*bows his head low and with folded hands*)

Juhaar, master!

Dina: Alright! Juhaar!

Haebo boy,

You have become a great man, can't even recognize my voice?

Hadu: Don't mock me, master?

Dina: Am I mocking you?

If I speak the truth, you feel I am mocking!

Hadu: If not mocking, then what are you hinting at? master, what did you notice that you called me a great man?

Dina: Calling a great man great sounds fiddly to you. Strange generation!

Hadu: Why did you repeat that?

Master, how far can the house lizard go?

The highest reach of a lizard could be the tip of the tenda.

Dina: This is not the common lizard, this is the high-yielding variety.

Hadu: (*smiles*) I feel like laughing as loud as the sound of the bursting of the big fat frog of the fairy tales,

Ha... ha... ha

Dina: Of course, you have become great people.

That is why I have received a wire, cablegram, telegram for you.

Hadu: Cable, wire?

How much cable do you want?

We have bhars filled with cable wires.

Do you mean cable to dry towels?

Dina: Not the cable to dry towels!

Cablegram...

Hadu: Cablegram?

Dina: Yes... cablegram. A letter.

Hadu: Who has sent it?

Show me.

Dina: (*gives the letter to Hadu*)

This letter is from our learned babu.

Hadu: (*looks at the letter*)

It looks very nice master, but, what shall I do with it?

It is like playing music for a deaf.

Dina: Can't you read and write?

Hadu: If I could read, I would not have waited till now without reading it.

Dina: Oh!

Hadu: How could I read and write?

My father always persuaded me to go school, but I didn't listen to him.

My father threw away my school bag along with the black slate board.

Dina: Not everyone is lucky in this world to get an education, Hadu dada.

Hadu: Whether it is in luck or not, is a different matter.

I was dull and lethargic in my studies from the beginning,

I always made excuses for stomachaches and headaches to escape from my studies.

Dina: Children play many such pranks in childhood.

Hadu: Life is playing pranks on me today for the pranks I played on life in childhood.

Dina: (*laughs*) Your words can make a mirthless man laugh, Hadu.

Hadu: Alright. You didn't tell me what the learned babu has written in the letter.

Dina: Yes, I will tell you.
(*reads the letter*) He writes that he has submitted his research papers to the government.
The government will soon have a discussion and take a decision on it.

Hadu: Learned babu is a good person.
Can the government dare not to listen to his matter?

Dina: Hadu, learned babu also writes that he is coming to this village.

Hadu: It would be nice if he can come today.

Dina: He has written that he will come today itself.

Hadu: Is it?

Dina: Truly!

Hadu: Swear on your mother.

Dina: I swear on my mother!

Hadu: In that case, it is going to be a grand celebration.

Dina: Let it be grand!
Let's have a grand celebration!

Hadu: It can be grand, but what can be done?
The drought this year, It is affecting all affairs and enjoyment.

Dina: Ehh!

I am here for you, why slow down the celebration till the time I am with you?

Hadu: Swear on your mother!

Dina: Truly!

If you are with us, then we don't have any scarcity. The more the better.

(*both laugh*)

Dina: You go and inform Aentha, Paltu and Gahadu about this letter.

Hadu: Alright, I am going. (*leaves*)

Dina: Listen, give this message to our sister Kasturi too.

Hadu: Ehhh! I will give this message first to our nuni Kasturi.

I am going brother, will tell everyone, that our learned babu is coming today.

Dina: Go soon. We will give him a grand welcome to the village.

All expenses on me, celebrate it splendidly.

(*leaves*)

Hadu: We will shower him with garlands of flower.

Whatever may be, learned babu is coming right on the occasion of the harvest festival.

I will give this message first to Kasturi, and these people have already gone to get chher-chhera, I shall go...

(*Hadu runs away, Kasturi returns home through the village along with Aentha. Both enter home. Aentha comes out holding his Muhuri.*)

Aentha: Nuni Kasturi, bring the rope cot from home and put it here.

Kasturi: (*from inside the house*)
I will bring it.

(*Kasturi brings the rope cot and places it there. Sitting on the cot, Aentha plays music on his Muhuri.*)

Kasturi: (*comes to Aentha*)
Don't blow the Muhuri so high, dada.

Aentha: I have spent my entire life playing this Muhuri, nuni.

Kasturi: You have played as much as you can so far, stop it now.
Look at yourself once, your ribcage looks strange.

Aentha: Do you think, I have pierced my chest by blowing this Muhuri?
No, nuni, will you understand the inner feelings and thoughts of my mind, nuni?
What do you know?

I was a very handsome attractive young man.

Looking at my sturdy muscular physique, everyone used to say that a giant has taken birth.

Truly, I have long hands like a giant broad large chest. The muscles of my brawny arms were strong as iron.

The earth thudded with the sounds of my heavy footsteps.

But of what use?

I failed, I couldn't do anything for you all.

Phula's mother, poor thing, could not get any happiness in her life.

She died young leaving me insecure and helpless (*cries*)

Here you are, the only one I have with me, yet, I could not give you any happiness.

I could not provide you with even a handful to eat and proper clothing.

You were blessed by God with the virtue and beauty of a high born, but low-born in a destitute family. (*coughs*)

Kasturi: Keep quiet dada!

Aentha: This rascal god is very bad.

His creation is amiss. Here I am, a bloody drunkard. I get so high after I start drinking, that I can't control myself and what I say.

Just a few pegs make me blind drunk and I fail to see even god, the Sun, Moon, mother, sister.

I have scolded, beaten and tortured you too much.

My life is dreadful pathetic.

I am alive just because I am not dead.

I wish I die soon, nuni.

Kasturi: Oh, dada, why do you feel bad?

Who says you didn't do anything for us?

Aentha: What have I done for you?

Is there any worthless person like me in this world?

Kasturi: Dada, it is because of you that we live like a king.

Do we have any kind of scarcity in our life that makes you feel bad?

Aentha: No matter how much you try to console me,

I can see through it all.

Kasturi: You don't talk any more.

Can't you see you are panting while talking?

Aentha: Whatever is happening let it happen.

What can we do?

(*Hadu arrives shouting*)

Aentha: Why are you shouting, Hadu?

Hadu: Learned babu is arriving today.
He has written a letter to wealthy Dina.

Aentha: What did you say?

Hadu: Learned babu is arriving today.
He has written a letter to wealthy Dina.
He told me just now.

Aentha: Who?
Learned babu is coming?
Swear on your mother?

Hadu: Dada, I swear on my mother!
Truly, nuni!

Aentha: (*happily*) The learned babu is coming,
Kasturi, your learned babu is coming.

(*Kasturi goes inside shyly*)

Hadu: Wealthy Dina has said, no matter the cost, we will give a grand welcome to the learned babu.

Aentha: Haebo Hadu, come here, sit with me.

(*Hadu sits on the cot close to Aentha*)

Hadu, fortune favoured our Kasturi,

(*smiles happily*)

God Ramchandra is coming back to our village.
Hadu, where are Gahadu, Maharagu and Paltu?
They should be here at such moments.

Hadu: They have gone to get chher-chhera brother. Gahadu has taken away my musical instrument along with him.

Aentha: Go and call them.

Hadu: I am going to bring all of them here.

Aentha: Run along.

Hadu: (*while he leaves*)

Dada...

(*Music is heard*)

Here they are.

Come quickly.

(*Maharagu, Gahadu, Paltu and Hurshi along with Phula arrive playing music. Aentha holds the Muhuri.*)

Aentha: Hey Maharagu, Gahadu, Paltu, our learned babu will come today.

Play some music.

Maharagu: Swear on your mother?

Gahadu: You swear?

Paltu: Is the learned babu coming?

All: Ho... (*Aentha dances while playing the Muhuri. All of them dance. Kasturi comes out holding a basket of flowers.*)

Kasturi: Brother, don't blow your Muhuri very high.

Your chest is weak.

Aentha: Nuni, don't stop me today.
I am very happy today.
Hey... why did you stop?
Play on!

Maharagu: (*to Hadu*)
You midget.

Hadu: Yes!

Maharagu: What are you waiting for?
Sing a song!

(*All play the music and sing. Kasturi weaves garland of flowers seated on the verandah.*)

Hadu: (*sings*)
Oh dear!
An honourable shoulder deserves the sacred thread
A beautiful mind deserves a noble husband.
I wish on such an auspicious occasion
I get my desired beloved!
Oh dear!
The exquisite anklets add to the grace of the feet
The alluring postiche adds to the charm of the hair bun
Life has become a tough row to hoe,
Yet my mind plays a jolly tune.

Oh dear!
You deceived me with your illusory skills
I wish to have fun and frolic with you,
I wish my beloved sways in golden swings.

Paltu: (*sings*)
Walking on Nature's trail,
I came across a rat snake.

Hurshi: (*sings*)
Rasarkeli re!
O juicy fruit!
Hey boys,
I went fishing to the river Mahanadi
Caught a variety of bony fish
A young girl is cooking fish,
With her captivating curvy hips.

Maharagu: (*sings*)
Oh, adorable Krishna,
Come and sit with me.
This flower is not luscious
You were oblivious
Now that you are aware
Move away from this flower
My gold belly chain is beguiling
Oh! My goldsmith boy.

Aentha: Oh! God Rama...

All: God Rama...

Aentha: (*sings*)

Paddy plant growing loaded with bunches of paddies.

Come back soon our learned babu.

Take away our nuni along with you.

(*Song and dance continue for a while. Dina comes running and shouting.*)

Dina: Aentha dada!

(*All of them stopped singing and dancing. They all were silent for a while. Phula goes to her nana, Kasturi. Dina reaches them panting.*)

Aentha dada!

Aentha: What happened, master?

Dina: Our learned babu...
No... no...
It is nothing.

Aentha: What happened to our learned babu?

Maharagu: Master, what happened?

(*Dina whispers something into Maharagu's ears. All look at Maharagu. Maharagu sits down looking broken. He doesn't speak to anyone.*)

Aentha: Master, what happened to our learned babu?
Tell us.
(*gets angry*)
Haebo Maharagu, why don't you tell me?
What happened to our learned babu?

Maharagu: (*stands up, cries*)
Police have taken our learned babu into custody,
But it is not known why he has been taken into custody.

Dina: The learned babu was doing his research on the folk dancers, folk singers, and folk musicians moving across all villages.
He collected information from all these people for his research work.
The objective of his research was to understand and analyse the customs, traditions and way of living of these people.
However, having stayed amongst you, he wrote in his research about the 'haves and have-nots'.
The difference that is prevalent between the rich and the poor.
He must have mentioned something in his research, which went against the government!
Why should he not write?
Who will write about these people then?

Is the government even doing anything for these people?

He didn't fight with anyone, didn't harm anyone, nor did he rob.

What has he written that the government considered him a gangster, rogue, traitor, and pushed him into jail?

If by telling truth he is sent to jail, let it be!

We all will go to jail along with him.

How many can they push into jail,

Let them do it!

(While listening to this, Aentha feels more the intense pain in his chest. He plays sad tunes and blows his Muhuri high with tears streaming down his eyes. All sit down with their Muhuria and look at him. He keeps blowing his Muhuri and at the end vomits blood.)

Hadu: Ibua! What happened to Guru?

Paltu: Too much blood!

Maharagu: Give him some fresh air, bring some water, nuni.

Dina: I will bring it.

(While bringing water in a coconut shell, Dina slips and falls breaking the shell. Then, Gahadu brings some water.)

Gahadu: Here it is, drink some water.

Maharagu: Aentha dada, drink some water. *(Helps him drink)*

Kasturi: Imaa!

What has happened to my brother?

(holds Phula)

Dada, look at her, who is she?

Do you recognize her?

Dada, tell me, who is she?

(While drinking water, Aentha succumbs to death. Kasturi cries loudly.)

What did you do to me, dada? You have devastated me.

(Phula cries even loudly)

Dina: Hurshi, you take Phula out somewhere.

(Hurshi takes away Phula and goes towards the village. Maharagu, Paltu, Hadu and Gahadu lay Aentha straight and cover him with a towel. All start shedding tears. Dina consoles everyone.)

Hadu: Wealthy dada, how can Aentha dada leave us forever?

Dina: Since morning, my left eye had been twitching. I was quite apprehensive that something unfortunate might happen, a great mishap.

Hadu: What shall we do now?

I feel like I'm losing my mind.

Dina: He was a very nice person.

Maharagu: He was our Guru, a great musician.

Dina: Everyone will leave this world one day.

Paltu: Everyone will leave – nobody is born with the crown of immortality.

Hadu: Wealthy dada, will the dead body be left lying like this?

Dina: Why shall the dead body be left lying like that? We all are here. We will pick up the dead body and give him a proper cremation. I am going home to change my dhoti for the funeral.

Hadu: Alright dada!

Dina: (*sees Kasturi crying*)

Dear Kasturi, why do you cry?

Your brother died and left you behind, does that mean you will keep crying like this?

Am I not a brother to you?

Why do you worry till the time I am alive?

Wealthy Dina is here for you.

You have everything.

(*Kasturi starts blubbering*)

Nuni Kasturi, learned babu will come back to you. At present, he is in jail, but someday, the government will release him.

My heart says the learned babu can never forget you. He will surely come back to you.

He will put a garland around your neck and accept you as his wife.
Don't cry, dear. (*leaves*)

(*Dina leaves the stage and walks towards the village. Maharagu, Paltu, Hadu and Gahadu get busy arranging things for funeral pyre and cremation rituals. They place the rope cot upside down and lay the dead body of Aentha on the cot. They anoint the corpse with oil and turmeric. A song is heard from inside the house*: 'Whether the fallen fresh leaves decay in water or not...' *Dina arrives with rice straw ropes, a bamboo basket filled with popped rice and a new piece of long cloth, for funeral rituals. He removes the towel covering on the corpse's body and covers it with the new cloth. After that, they pick up the cot from all four sides. Kasturi cries loudly not to take her brother away from her. They all leave carrying the corpse. Dina accompanies them throwing popped rice and chants 'Ram Naam Satya Hai' loudly while carrying the corpse for the funeral. Kasturi keeps looking at the colour of the sunrise and the song heard from inside gradually comes to an end.*)

Song: The leaves fallen in water may or may not decay,
But it decays the water.
What is your fault,
Oh, my precious dear.
With pain your heart tears.
The leaves fallen in water may or may not decay,
But it decays the water.

I didn't die,
How could 'Yama' take you away?
The leaves fallen in water may or may not decay,
But it decays the water.
People come and leave this world
We commemorate with mithibhaat.
The leaves fallen in water may or may not decay,
But it decays the water.
You were the gem of this village my dear
The village reminisces about you; everyone misses you,
Remembers you.

Lights off. Stage is dark

Scene V

(Kasturi keeps looking at the colour of the sky of the rising sun. While the song gets over, she turns back and hears Phula calling her from inside the house.)

Phula: Haego nana, come and give me something to eat.

Kasturi: (*loudly*) Coming... (*goes inside the hut*)

(*Sun rises and the play ends*)

The curtain falls.

Glossary

Arsa pitha: It is a traditional sweet made in Odisha. It is flat and round with its outer layer is crispy whereas the inner layer is soft. It is made of rice flour, jaggery, sesame seeds and clarified butter.

Babu: This word is used in India as a respectful title or form of address for a gentleman, especially an educated man; a term of respect attached to a proper name. It is used to mean 'sir' while addressing a gentleman. It is also used as a term of respect for any elder man.

Bajnia: An orchaestra that plays traditional folk music with traditional musical instruments in villages of western Odisha.

Bhaar: It is a pair of bamboo baskets balanced on a carrying pole (also called shoulder pole, a yoke of wood or bamboo) used by people to carry a load. The two baskets are tied to the two opposite sides of the bamboo poles with ropes. The basket is broad at the top and usually tapered at its base. People in the Indian villages carry it by hanging and balancing the yoke on one or both the shoulders, and the baskets with loads being suspended and tied with ropes to the pole.

Bhama: Name of an imaginary girl referred to in the folk song in the play.

Bhukha: A starved person

Chandra: He is considered as the God of Moon in Hindu religion in Indian mythology.

Chher-chhera: A custom of sharing grains during Puspuni, the harvest festival of the year that is celebrated on a full moon's night in January. People from all ages form their groups and go to each and every house in the village, singing the song of joy and demand for grains to the lady of the house. The festival is a symbol of bonding, gratitude, merry-making and prosperity.

Dada: An elder brother or a friendly form of address for a man. In Sambalpuri, the term is also used as an affectionate form of address to an older person

Dalkhai: It is a popular folk song of Sambalpur, in western Odisha.

Dhoti: It is a traditional Indian male dress, comprising a cotton white long unstitched loincloth. It is worn by men in India to cover. It is wrapped around the waist that extends to the lower part, covering most of the legs.

Ganda: The Ganda are an indigenous scheduled caste community in Odisha. The Gandas are best known for their special music known as Ganda Baja, which is essential for village functions throughout western Odisha.

Gauntia: A person who was selected by a king as the chief of the village in the feudal system in western Odisha. His role was to collect revenue from the village people. He was the wealthiest man of the village and usually from the upper caste.

Guru: In India, a spiritual leader or teacher in the Hindu religion. A mentor, guide, expert, or master of certain knowledge or field is addressed as Guru

Haebo: A common informal form of address to a male friend in Sambalpuri.

Haego: A common informal form of address to an intimate/close elder person in Sambalpuri

Huzoor: A title of respect for a person of high rank in the Indian feudal system

Ibua: An interjection or exclamation in Sambalpuri

Imaa: An interjection or exclamation in Sambalpuri

Indra: He is considered as the god of war and weather; also, the King of the gods in the heaven in Hindu religion and mythology.

Jama: He is the god of death in Hindu religion and mythology.

Jarasandha: He was the king of Magadha and the son of King Brihadratha. He is an antagonist in the epic Mahabharata. He was born from two mothers and one father. Each mother gave birth to one half of him (the upper half of his body came from one mother and the lower half by another). A demoness named Jara picked up these two halves by holding each piece in each of her palm and joined them together in the shape of a child. The child got life and was named Jarasandh, after the name of the Demoness Jara and Sandha in Sanskrit, which means 'joining'). The dramatis personae in the play, while having a verbal fight with another person, refer to Jarasandha in the context that he will rip him apart separating the body into two halves like the two halves of the body of Jarasandha.

Jhilliparagi: It is a variety of paddy rice grown in western Odisha, known for its good qualities such as aroma, lightweight, fine texture, nutritious with good taste and flavour.

Juhaar: Amongst the Hindus in Sambalpur, it is a customary non-contact manner of respectfully greeting and honouring a person/group with folded hands and joined palms.

Karat: It is a round coin storage box mostly made of silver. It is usually used by women in villages in western Odisha.

Kenti: Name of an imaginary girl referred to in the folk song in the play

Kurta: A long loose collarless shirt that extends up to the thighs and worn by men in India

Lakshmi: She is the goddess of wealth and prosperity in the Hindu mythology.

Mahabharata: The Mahabharata is a Sanskrit epic of ancient India. It narrates the story of the war between two groups of cousins' princes, the Kaurava and the Pāṇḍava.

Mahanadi: River that flows through Sambalpur

Mithibhaat: A custom in the villages in Sambalpur in which all family members, friends and relatives are invited to eat a meal together in remembrance of the deceased after the funeral

Nana: (Aunt) The sister of one's father in Sambalpuri.

Nuni: A female child/adolescent/young or relatively young woman in Sambalpuri

Pajama: Loose cotton trousers or pants worn by Indian men. It is tied around the waist and covers the legs till toes.

Pupchi, Sualin, Dudra, Manda, Kanda Phulki: Varieties of sweets made in Western Odisha

Puspuni: It is a traditional annual harvest festival celebrated in western Odisha on the full moon day in the month of January, after the harvest of kharif paddy. People offer newly harvested paddy to god and celebrate with music, dance, food and drinks.

Ramachandra: He is an incarnation of God Vishnu in Hindu religion and mythology. Also, he is the hero of the epic Ramayana. He is worshipped for his truth, honesty, commitment, self-sacrifice, courage, and purity.

Rasarkeli: It is a famous folk song of Sambalpur in western Odisha.

Saptapar: A traditional design of saree in Sambalpur, western Odisha.

Sita: A goddess in Hindu mythology. She is the female protagonist of the Hindu epic, Ramayana. She is the wife of God Ramachandra and known for her dedication, self-sacrifice, and courage.

Shakuntala: Name of an imaginary girl referred to in the folk song in the play

T.B.: It is the abbreviation for the disease Tuberculosis.

Tenda: It is a traditional system to draw water from open wells that is still practiced even today in Odisha. It functions on the simple principles of lever. Tenda is efficient than the traditional pulley-and-rope system (or windlasses).